FEARLESS CITIES

FEARLESS CITIES

A Guide to the Global Municipalist Movement

Compiled by
Barcelona En Comú
Contributions from
Debbie Bookchin,
Ada Colau et al

New Internationalist

Fearless Cities:
A Guide to the Global Municipalist Movement

First published in 2019 by
New Internationalist Publications Ltd
The Old Music Hall
106-108 Cowley Road
Oxford
OX4 1JE, UK
newint.org

Design and cover design: Juha Sorsa

Printed by T J International Limited, Cornwall, UK
who hold environmental accreditation ISO 14001.

British Library Cataloguing-in-Publication Data
A catalogue record for this book is available from the British Library.

Library of Congress Cataloging-in-Publication Data
A catalog record for this book is available from the Library of Congress.

ISBN 978-1-78026-503-2
(ebook ISBN 978-1-78026-504-9)

Contents

Policy toolkits

Introduction

Gerardo Pisarello and the International Committee of Barcelona en Comú

THIS BOOK is a guide to a global movement, written by the people who are building it, street by street. It's a movement known by many names, from Fearless (or Rebel) Cities, to Cities of Change, Indy Towns, *neomunicipalismo*, democratic confederalism, communalism and our own preferred term, municipalism. This varied nomenclature is, in itself, a reflection of who we are: decentralized, diverse and radically pragmatic.

Here in Barcelona, as we write these lines, our city hall is run by former housing rights activist Ada Colau, who was elected mayor in 2015. This book is the result of a process of international collaboration, sparked by the surprise election victory of our municipalist platform, Barcelona En Comú, that year.

From the moment we took office, Barcelona En Comú has been mapping and exchanging experiences with over a hundred municipalist organizations from around the world. These organizations have been working to support one another in pursuit of shared goals. In June 2017, we all came together for the first time for the first municipalist summit, 'Fearless Cities', in Barcelona. That event, which gathered over 700 participants, from every continent, was a turning point. It was living proof that we are not alone; that each individual municipalist initiative forms part of an emerging global movement that transcends local and national borders.

More than a destination, this guide is the next step in this journey. *Fearless Cities: A Guide to the Global Municipalist Movement* doesn't aim to be an encyclopedia of municipalism. Rather, it provides a snapshot of the concerns and activities of a movement that's in a constant state of growth and evolution. It's the first, inevitably incomplete, attempt to document this informal network of organizations around the world, which, to relatively little fanfare, has been transforming towns and cities from the bottom up.

At the back of the book, you'll find a map of the global municipalist movement and a directory of 50 municipalist organizations from 19 countries around the world that have been actively collaborating with Barcelona En Comú and with one another. This section, while by no means exhaustive, gives a sense of the geographical scope and diversity of the movement as it stands today.

Indeed, in many ways, this publication is a tangible example of the municipalist movement in action. It has been written by over 144 contributors from 54 towns and cities, the majority of them women. It's the product of a collective, horizontal process, bringing together the knowledge and experience of mayors, councillors and grassroots activists so as to share the story of municipalism with the world.

The four chapters in Section One aim to answer the questions 'What is municipalism?' and 'How can municipalism radicalize democracy, feminize politics and provide alternatives to the far right?'

One of the defining characteristics of municipalism is its conviction that the 'how' of politics is just as important as the 'what'. The organizing toolkits in Section Two provide advice on how to create participatory candidacies and how to build the alternative practices, priorities and power structures we want to see in the world in our own organizations.

While any attempt to define a standard municipalist policy agenda would be contrary to the decentralized, autonomous nature of the movement, it is true that the local sphere tends to put particular political issues at the centre of the public debate. While the legal powers and responsibilities of local governments around the world vary, invariably local politics centres on concrete issues that affect people's daily lives. The policy toolkits in Section Three explore just some of the main issues on the municipalist agenda at the moment, such as housing, public space and local economies.

There are three dimensions of municipalism that we consider so fundamental that we have featured them throughout the book. The first is the feminization of politics, which involves both questioning patriarchal models of organization and power and putting care work at the centre of both the political agenda and modes of organization. So vital is this aspect of municipalism that you will find a section dedicated to it in almost every chapter of this book.

The second cross-cutting aspect of municipalism is its focus on concrete action. We believe that the best political argument consists of small victories that prove things can be done differently, from both inside and outside local institutions. With this in mind, we have included over 50 examples of transformative local practices, tools and policies that can serve as inspiration and guides for action.

Finally, this guide is testament to the internationalist commitment of the municipalist movement. Though municipalists prioritize local organizing, action and solutions, this should by no means be interpreted as a retreat into selfishness or parochialism. We are all too aware of the global nature of the challenges we face in our neighbourhoods, and we believe that we can only meet them by working together. That's why the book features a number of examples of how municipalist organizations, towns and cities are working as networks to take on global challenges.

Last but not least, we would like to point out how this movement is growing and spreading far and wide – the first 'Fearless Cities' gathering in Barcelona was just that: the first. Since then many other similar initiatives have been using municipalism to think about and organize their work, including regional Fearless Cities summits, mutual support for campaigns, local conferences, and many other events that reflect on culture, environment or social rights from the municipalist standpoint.

We hope you will find this book inspiring and, above all, useful. In order to win Barcelona for the common good, we need other people around the world to act in the same way: to come together with their neighbours, to imagine alternatives for their town or city, and to start to build them from the bottom up. This is just the beginning.

WHAT IS MUNICIPALISM?

1

The future we deserve

Debbie Bookchin, writer and journalist

I AM the daughter of two long-time municipalists.

My mother, Beatrice Bookchin, ran for the City Council of Burlington, Vermont, in 1987 on a municipalist platform of building an ecological city, a moral economy and, above all, citizen assemblies that would contest the power of the nation-state. My father is the social theorist and libertarian municipalist Murray Bookchin.

For many years the Left has struggled with the question of how to bring our ideas – of equality, economic justice and human rights – to fruition. And my father's political trajectory is instructive for the argument that I want to make: that municipalism isn't just one of many ways to bring about social change, it is really the only way that we will successfully transform society.

As someone who had grown up as a young communist and been deeply educated in Marxist theory, my father became troubled by the economistic, reductionist modes of thinking that had historically permeated the Marxist Left. He was searching for a more expansive notion of freedom – not just freedom from economic exploitation, but freedom from all manner of oppressions: race, class, gender, ethnicity.

At the same time, in the early 1960s, it became increasingly clear to him that capitalism was on a collision course with the natural world. Murray believed you could not address environmental problems piecemeal – trying to save redwood forests one day, and opposing a nuclear power plant the next – because ecological stability was under attack by capitalism.

That is to say, the profit motive, the grow-or-die ethos of capitalism, was fundamentally at odds with the ecological stability of the planet.

So he began to elaborate this idea that he called social ecology, which starts from the premise that all ecological problems are social problems. Murray said that, in order to heal our rapacious relationship with the natural world, we must fundamentally alter social relations – we have to end not only class oppression but also domination and hierarchy at every level, whether it be the domination of women by men, of lesbians, gays and transgender people by straights, of people of colour by whites, or of the young by the old.

So the question for him became: how do we bring a new egalitarian society into being? What type of alternative social organization will create a society in which truly emancipated human beings can flourish and heal our rift with the natural world? The question really is: what kind of political organization can best contest the power of the state?

And so, in the late 1960s, Murray began writing about a form of organization that he called libertarian municipalism.

He believed that municipalism offered a third way out of the deadlock between the Marxist and anarchist traditions. Municipalism rejects seizing state power, which we all know from looking at the example of the Soviet Union is a hopeless pursuit, a dead end, because the state, whether capitalist or socialist, with its faceless bureaucracy, is never responsive to the people.

And, at the same time, activists must acknowledge that we won't achieve social change simply by taking our demands to the street. Large encampments and demonstrations may challenge the authority of the state, but they have not succeeded in usurping it. Those who engage only in a politics of protest or organizing on the margins of society must recognize that there will always be power – it does not simply dissolve. The question is, in whose hands will power reside – in those of the state, with its centralized authority, or in those of the people at the local level?

It is increasingly clear that we will never achieve the kind of

13

fundamental social change we so desperately need simply by going to the ballot box. Social change won't be brought about by voting for the candidate who promises us a $15 minimum wage, free education or family leave, or who offers platitudes about social justice. When we confine ourselves to voting for the least of many evils, to the bones that social democracy throws our way, we play into and support the centralized state structure that is designed to keep us down forever.

And, though often overlooked by the Left, there is a rich history of directly democratic politics, of citizen self-government: from Athens [in Ancient Greece], to the Paris Commune, to the Anarchist collectives of Spain in 1936, to Chiapas, Mexico, to Barcelona and other Spanish cities and towns in recent years, and now to Rojava, in Syria, where the Kurdish people have implemented a profoundly democratic project of self-rule unlike anything ever seen in the Middle East.

A municipalist politics is about much more than bringing a progressive agenda to City Hall – important as that may be. Municipalism, or communalism, as my father called it, returns politics to its original definition – a moral calling based on rationality, community, creativity, free association and freedom. It is a richly articulated vision of a decentralized democracy in which people act together to chart a rational future. At a time when human rights, democracy and the public good are under attack by increasingly nationalistic, authoritarian, centralized state governments, municipalism allows us to reclaim the public sphere for the exercise of authentic citizenship and freedom.

Municipalism demands that we return power to ordinary citizens, that we reinvent what it means to do politics and what it means to be a citizen. True politics is the opposite of parliamentary politics. It begins at the base, in local assemblies. It is transparent, with candidates who are 100-per-cent accountable to their neighbourhood organizations, who are delegates rather than wheeling-and-dealing representatives. It celebrates the power of local assemblies to transform, and be transformed by, an increasingly enlightened citizenry. And it is celebratory – in the very act of doing politics we become new human beings, we build an alternative to capitalist modernity.

Municipalism asks key questions. What does it mean to be a human being? What does it mean to live in freedom? How do we organize society in ways that foster mutual aid, caring and co-operation?

These questions and the politics that follow from them carry an ethical imperative – not only because we must live in harmony with the natural world or we destroy the basis for life itself, but also because we have a moral imperative to maximize equality and freedom.

The great news is that this politics is being articulated more and more vocally in horizontalist movements around the world. In the factory-recuperation politics of Argentina, in the water wars of Bolivia, in the neighbourhood councils that have arisen in Italy, where the government was useless in assisting municipalities after severe flooding: over and over we see people organizing at the local level to take power, indeed to create a countervailing power that increasingly challenges the power and authority of the nation-state.

These movements are taking the idea of democracy and expressing it to its fullest potential, creating a politics that meets human needs, that fosters sharing and co-operation, mutual aid and solidarity, and that recognizes women must play a leadership role.

Achieving this means taking our politics into every corner of our neighbourhoods, doing what the conservatives around the world have done so successfully in the past few decades: running candidates at the municipal level.

It also means creating a minimum programme – such as ending home foreclosures [the repossession of mortgaged homes by banks], stopping escalating rents and the destabilization of our neighbourhoods through gentrification. But we should also develop a maximum programme, in which we re-envision what society could be if we could build a caring economy, harness new technologies, and expand the potential of every human being to live in freedom and exercise their civic rights as members of flourishing, truly democratic communities.

And we must confederate, work across state and national borders, developing programmes that will address regional and even international issues. This is an important response to those who say that we won't be able to solve great transnational problems by acting at the local level. In fact, it is precisely at the local level where these problems are being solved day in and day out. Even great issues such as climate change can be managed through the confederation of communities that send delegates to manage regional and even transcontinental issues. We don't need a centralized state bureaucracy.

We need to create lasting political institutions at the local level, not merely politicians who articulate a social-justice agenda. We need institutions that are directly democratic, egalitarian, transparent, fully accountable, anti-capitalist and ecologically aware and that give voice to the aspirations of the people. It will require time and education and the building of municipal assemblies as a countervailing power to the nation-state, but this is our only hope of becoming the new human beings needed to build a new society.

This is our time. Around the world people want not merely to survive but to live. If we are to transition from the death-spiral society that decades of neoliberalism have foisted upon us to a new rational society that delivers on the promise of humankind, we must create a global network of fearless cities, towns and villages. We deserve nothing less.

2

New life begins at the local level

Jorge Sharp, Mayor of Valparaíso

THERE IS no denying that Valparaíso is a special city, as port towns often are: open to the winds that bring in different types of people. But Valparaíso also stands out for its history; for its tradition of collective action in co-operatives and at the dawn of unionism; for its striking coastline, made up of hills and ravines, covered in houses painted all the colours of the rainbow – colours chosen freely by the headstrong folk who live there.

Valparaíso, Chile's second city, is also a politically complex space, defined by the actions of undemocratic powers that had left the municipality drowning in debt and unable to deal with its many problems. It is a city that had been abandoned, a city crumbling to pieces due to regular fire outbreaks and poverty.

In December 2016 we humbly took office in the local government. We were mostly representatives of a citizens' movement and of political groupings that were determined to put to an end a succession of incompetent, insensitive and occasionally corrupt local administrations. Many of us had participated in the formidable student movements that shook the foundations of the country's political and economic model in 2011-12. It was a coming together of distinct political and social currents that would take charge of the local government. But we did not know how to govern. We did not have the experience, or enough professionals, or enough trained technicians. What we did have was decisiveness, a sense of solidarity and support from the rest of the country and beyond, and the will to work tirelessly for change.

What also got us into this position was our desire to develop a local political project. When we began to organize and prepare to stand for election in Valparaíso, there had been little debate on the role of local politics in Chilean political organizations. The experience of the successful student movement tended to tip the balance significantly in favour of issue-based approaches.

While we may not have been the only people identifying the need to revitalize local and territorial politics, it was we who were able to actually make it happen through our victory in the municipal elections of October 2016, hot on the heels of the 'citizen primaries' that we had organized earlier that same year. Today there is no doubt about the relevance of local politics in Chile.

However, we had never understood municipal politics as being opposed to or excluding of the national sphere. Chile is an extremely centralized country, with deep-rooted oligarchic tendencies; it is a strong presidential regime that is inclined, as one might expect from a neoliberal polity, towards negotiation with great world economic powers and global financial institutions; local autonomy is extremely constrained and, as decisions are taken in the capital, so wealth is generated centrally as well. In a context such as this, it is impossible to think about local strategies without taking national politics into account, let alone to accept the local political and administrative borders drawn under the military dictatorship. Indeed, many of the problems we face today have their origins in the false decentralization of the 1980s.

In this context, local political work is revealed as fundamental, both in the transforming practice of local government and in the revitalization of local communities. And this is where we can make clear progress in rebuilding communities and in connecting mobilizations and protests to the construction of new forms of life which are fuller and more egalitarian, here and now. The territorial community, however nascent it may currently be, is in our experience capable of creating and enacting alternative forms of daily life, leading to less commodified social relations becoming less commodified, to fairer coexistence between equals, and to a living and concrete project for the future.

Our key tool is participation. I say 'tool', but it is more than that: participation is in itself the putting-into-practice of a desire for equality, for democracy, for the fellowship of humanity.

So we seek to build new and better ways of living, and to best manage the resources of the city in order to improve the lives of all who live in it. Maybe this means establishing a pharmacy that sells medicines for no profit, or perhaps an optician's that can both carry out eye tests and obtain cheap lenses. The next project for us is a laboratory that can carry out simple medical analyses, and the one after that the provision of houses that are fireproofed to a notably higher degree than standard social housing.

These are institutional initiatives that can lower some of the steepest costs that make the neoliberal model so expensive for people, and which have transformed Chile into one of the most unequal societies on the planet.

But we want more than this. Alongside these efforts to provide accessible services, and step by step to improve the immediate conditions of life in the city, we also want to make communities more dynamic and participative, to have people take the solutions to their problems into their own hands. We want to enable them to imagine the city they want and to build it, with the municipal structures as an instrument to help them achieve their aims. It is here that our local political project will achieve its greatest value and reach.

We face global challenges. We are well aware of this and try to think at a global level. The old 'principal port' of the South Pacific still looks outwards and thinks of distant lands; it still confronts global trends in commerce and the transport of raw materials; it is still beaten down by speculation in real estate; it is still, without question, criss-crossed by the great challenges of contemporary capitalism: challenges which a local politics of social justice should not ignore, even for an instant. But we have also learnt both to speak from our own experience, and to delve into the reflections and discoveries of other men and women who have, like us, tried to blaze a trail to emancipate humanity, starting from its particular circumstances.

3

Feminizing politics through municipalism

Laura Pérez, Councillor Responsible for Feminism, LGBTI Affairs and International Relations, Barcelona City Council

HISTORY SHOWS us that feminism is invariably brave and transformative. This is so not just in terms of its relation to the outside world, generating public policies aimed at increasing equality between men and women, but also in terms of its capacity to examine itself and the organizations which seek to practise it. The social structures that surround us all and shape our daily lives need constant vigilance from us if we are to protect them. We must continually insist on the central importance of feminism and its teachings as a form of political practice, because this is the practical application of the old adage that without feminism there can be no revolution: without an intervention in daily life, in what is happening all the time, no real change is possible.

One of the fundamental questions therefore is this: how can we democratize our candidacies and municipal experiences from a feminist point of view? One of the answers in recent years is that we will do this 'by feminizing politics'. But defining what this means and making it happen will only be possible through collective action. What I will attempt to explain here is based on carrying out hundreds of conversations, reading hundreds of articles, making mistakes, getting things right – in short, from all the steps that have helped me create a collective idea of what a true feminization of politics might look like, and what the key steps are that we need to take in order to bring it about.

The first basic condition of action is parity of men and women in the spaces where politics takes place. Women's presence in these spaces is vital, precisely because we wish to end the marginalization of the knowledge and perspective of people who have been excluded from society and from political decision-making. With this in mind, we can point to several examples of municipalist movements outside Spain that have been clear about this from the start.

Consider, for example, the Kurdish municipalist movements, which are based on the idea of shared leadership, and which have carried this idea into practice all the way to the top, so that the position of mayor and the higher roles in government are never occupied solely by men. We in Barcelona En Comú are trying to follow this path. For example, our executive and administrative teams are collective and gender-balanced, and the team that governs the city is 60-per-cent female.

Another important step we have taken is to reduce vertical hierarchies and create mechanisms that harness collective intelligence and seek out the collectively generated knowledge that is too often appropriated by a small minority. We believe that all voices should be heard, and so we need to develop more horizontal and democratic ways of organizing our meetings: these include shorter speaking times, making sure it is not always the same people who speak, and ensuring that all decisions are taken collectively.

There are a large number of organizational studies which show that men tend to speak for longer and this usually leads to their enjoying increased legitimacy when it comes to taking decisions. This means we need to adopt practices in our meetings and assemblies such as alternating between giving the floor to men and women, or, if women are not speaking, saying so in order to acknowledge our lack of participation. These mechanisms are necessary in order to make inequalities visible and include our voices in democratic processes. For example, in our meetings we record how long men and women speak for to show the difference between them and to start to reduce it. This is an exercise that raises our awareness of things that usually happen unnoticed. Social movements such as 15M or the Women's March carry out similar practices.

We must also reconsider why we consider someone to be an expert. Must they have a university degree? Must they be a candidate for office or an official spokesperson? Must they always be the most well-known person from the movement? These issues are interesting from a municipalist perspective. For example, many of the people who participate in neighbourhood assemblies understand the daily reality of their communities and have knowledge that is extremely important for those of us who are in elected office and want to design public policies that work. Precisely because municipal problems are everyday problems, every resident is an expert on their neighbourhood. Their contributions must be put front and centre and treated as expert knowledge in such debates.

The third step is to work for a true sharing of responsibilities, political and personal, between men and women. This is probably the most difficult task that we face. Domestic tasks and caring roles are distributed extremely unevenly between women and men, with most of them falling to women. Guaranteeing women's participation in political action therefore depends to a great extent on the structure of society, on how people can organize their time, and on the inequalities in the social roles assigned to women and men. This, together with the pressure that the labour market puts on our ability to carve out personal time, makes it even more urgent and difficult for us to share responsibilities in our political activism.

In spite of all this, there are actions we can take within our organizations. For example, we can avoid scheduling meetings at the end of the working day; work to create spaces where children can also be present; invest organizational funds in play areas and child-friendly zones. We also need to take advantage of the opportunities offered by tools for digital participation, such as WhatsApp or Telegram, as well as the possibilities inherent in videoconferencing and mailing lists: these are all tools that can help us generate a working culture that respects our individual lives.

Finally, the fourth step to take is to incorporate gender equality as the lodestar of all our actions. When we ran in the 2015 municipal elections, we laid out the policies we were going to carry out, and did so collectively. As we thrashed out our policies, we were very clear that gender equality is not simply one more issue, that we weren't going to have a gender policy or a policy regarding LGBTI issues on one side, separate from our economic policy or our policies on mobility or urban development. Quite the opposite: gender equality, and the increasing democratic participation which we seek via the perspective of such issues as class, gender and social origins, has to be visible in every single one of the policies we put forward. Our aim is to permeate every single area of politics with a gender-oriented perspective, across the board.

An example of how we have done this in the Barcelona City Council is the way we drew up the municipal budget, taking into account its gender and neighbourhood impacts in order to be able to compensate for inequalities where necessary. We planned the transport network in the city taking into account the different ways in which men and women move around. Women still carry out most of the caring work (going shopping, taking children to school, going to hospital...) and so their travel round the city is different from that of men: gender is an important factor to include if we are to create truly equal policies.

When we design a city – its streets, buildings and the stories we tell about it – we also need to think about different needs and perspectives, and be aware that until now it has been male needs that have been considered the natural subjects and objects of political activity. When the government issues calls for tender, we have to include clauses related to gender parity, work-life balance, the pay gap and gender segregation in the companies we award contracts to.

This also has to be taken into account in a city's economic policy. We have to put people at the centre and recognize care work as essential to both life and the generation of wealth in society. This shift in perspective implies modifying public budgets to provide a collective response to the care needs that all of us have. These needs are felt throughout our lives and are currently barely recognized, largely because the work of meeting them fall on the shoulders of women, especially migrant women.

Being brave in politics today means accepting the fragility and interdependence of the human condition as the basis of all our action. It also involves rebelling against a system based on the false idea of individual omnipotence and the domination of the strongest over everyone else.

Feminizing politics means being realistic about our society's interpersonal and community needs, never forgetting that the ideal, strong individual, independent from the rest of the world, is actually dependent on the care of others, usually women.

If we want to achieve real transformation in the medium and long term, we cannot afford to lose our ability to imagine that transformation through feminism. We are going to work to make this happen because we want to live, fearless, and to participate in politics.

4

Standing up to the far right

Fátima Taleb, Councillor for Participation, Coexistence and Mediation, Badalona City Council

MY NAME is Fátima Taleb and I am an activist for the civil rights of Catalan people of foreign origin, as well as Councillor for Participation, Coexistence and Mediation in the Badalona City Council, and a member of the governing coalition, which comprises Guanyem Badalona, Esquerra Republicana and ICV-EUA.

I want to write about municipalism's capacity to oppose the far right, which sometimes hides behind rightwing, neoliberal parties.

In Badalona, the third most populous city in Catalonia, the rightwing Partido Popular (PP) government (2012–15) pursued exclusionary policies, advertised with slogans such as 'Let's clean up Badalona', or evidenced by the words of the former mayor, Xavier García Albiol, who said that 'native students are condemned to go to school alongside immigrants'. This was a display of ignorance, as it did not acknowledge the fact that a large proportion of those identified as 'immigrants' had been born and were being brought up in Spain. The PP transmitted messages very similar to those of far-right groups such as Plataforma por Catalunya, whose main slogan was 'Locals come first'.

The PP's actions in government were characterized by the closure of sites of worship (mainly for Muslims and Protestants), and the exclusion from local structures of social organization of those who did not support the governing party. It was a straightforwardly divisive policy, which aimed to generate a hostile climate towards all manifestations of diversity. Not only was it opposed to cultural diversity, but the PP government also refused to implement policies against discrimination on gender or disability, or supporting international solidarity.

All this took place during years of profound socioeconomic crisis, which generated insecurity among the people as they attempted to keep their jobs and their homes and to make loan payments; it was also a time of severe cuts in basic public services such as health and education. The far right took this opportunity to sow fear and to call for people to turn inwards: 'Danger comes from outside'; 'You have to defend yourselves'; 'Only we can protect you from these dangers', and so on.

The far right was directing itself towards a society which already has its share of stereotypes and xenophobic, racist and islamophobic elements. A breeding ground emerged in which people who once were prudent about making racist statements felt able to express those racist and discriminatory sentiments with impunity. This showed that the law in Spain is fundamentally unjust, as the courts' response to these statements was largely passive.

These messages got through to part of the population; their passage was made easier by an international context in which such figures as Trump, Putin and Le Pen are successful politicians. The aim of such messages is to create a scapegoat at the same level as those who perceive themselves as victims. 'It is your neighbour's fault; they are the ones taking your jobs, getting nice houses, getting bank loans.'

These sectors of the population do not realize that it is the population as a whole that is affected by these policies, which reduce individual liberty, increase state control and repression, and question the framework of human rights.

The far right, with its totalitarian tendencies and its striving towards homogenization, is profoundly anti-democratic, because democracy is based on the acknowledgement, respect and protection of all kinds of diversity. From the point of view of social cohesion, unity is not a synonym for uniformity. It is important to develop and apply a political philosophy based on fraternity and sorority, one that acknowledges how varied human experience can be, and which respects minorities. And this acknowledgement has to be based in a struggle against inequality, given that difference neither implies inequality nor a clash of binaries such as man-woman; local-foreigner; old-young.

I believe that municipalism is the ideal ground on which to stand up to the far right. It is in the close relations between citizens that discrimination is experienced, and where the fear of change is embodied. But also, it is at the local level – whether we are talking about cities where millions of people live, or towns of only a few hundred – that alternatives are created, and a truly communal way of living based on diversity comes into being. That is why we cannot make generalizations: not all the population is discriminatory or exclusive. There are people who think and act differently: it's why I am where I am today, brought here by the votes of brave citizens from my home town. And in return I promise to govern for everyone, irrespective of their origins or beliefs.

The far right can only be stopped on the streets, by being present in public and in private spaces; by promoting recognition based on mutual understanding between individuals. We have to promote the bonds between individuals: *if I know my neighbours I won't be afraid of them, and they won't be afraid of me*. These relationships, close and local, form a safety net that supports us when we fall, a set of connections based on fraternity/sorority, on the recognition of difference: siblings are different from each other, but they are connected by the ties of mutual dependency, as in a family. Even in times of conflict, which will always exist, these bonds allow for more constructive engagement. This is why we use family terms when we talk about members of our community: we say *tío* or *tía* (aunt or uncle), *primo*, *hermano* (cousin, brother) to people we are not related to. And remember too that the first-person-plural pronoun in Spanish, *nosotras*, contains within itself the key to diversity: *nos* ('we') and *otras* ('others').

This is why it is important to recover the idea of neighbourliness. To be a neighbour, we don't need to have papers that prove it: we just need to live in the same place as others. This is why we want to acknowledge citizenship by residency status, not by legal status or nationality. In spite of the legal obstacles put in place by laws such as those on foreign status or nationality, the European Statement on Human Rights in the City states that 'all cities which sign up to this document will extend the right to both active and passive suffrage on a municipal level to all citizens above the age of majority who are not national citizens, after a period of residence in the city of no less than two years'. Citizenship is the condition of all people who live in the city: they all have rights within the city and the rights of a citizen.

Fearless Cities are implementing local policies that aim for diversity while recognizing conflict. In Badalona, for example, we have reopened 'faith zones' after discussions with locals and after mediation with those opposed to the idea. And in order to counter the 'nimby' attitude of certain individuals, we have organized meetings throughout the city, such as the public *iftars* during last Ramadan, or the United Colours initiative. We want to show that the fear which divides us, the barriers between us, are all artificial, the product of messages that isolate us: there is nothing that makes us more afraid than feeling isolated, abandoned and excluded.

I am convinced that it is only through cities working together that it will be possible to transform society from the bottom up; through active citizenship. We need to create a new model of society which is fair, inclusive, inhabitable and which does not repress diversity but, on the contrary, sees it as one of the key elements of wealth and change. If we want to create real cities of change, or Fearless Cities, we need to include and fully recognize the rights of people of different cultural origins, different beliefs, different sexual orientations, different ages, genders, classes, ideologies, disabilities and so on. What I want is to apply an intersectional perspective to the issue.

Brave people, those who make a brave city, overcome their fear through mutual support, support from other brave people. It is only by making local communities strong and raising their awareness, making them brave, that we can resist and defeat totalitarianism and stand up to the far right.

ORGANIZING
TOOLKITS

5

How to create a participatory municipalist candidacy

Kate Shea Baird (Barcelona En Comú), **Claudia Delso** (Councillor for Participation and Democratic Innovation, A Coruña) and **Manuela Zechner** (researcher and cultural worker)

Creating a participatory municipalist platform isn't a question of marketing, it's a political question. It's not about creating policy through questionnaires, it's about creating a narrative that can mobilize a majority behind a project of transformation. The challenge isn't one of electoral strategy, it's one of meeting the concrete needs of sectors of the population who experience the contradictions of neoliberalism in our cities.

Jorge Sharp, Mayor of Valparaíso

Context

In 2010 and 2011 we occupied the squares to denounce politics-as-usual and to call for 'real democracy' for the 99 per cent. Together, we learned the value of open debate, collective intelligence, and horizontal, participatory decision-making (as well as their challenges!). For many of us, municipalism is a strategy that allows us to overcome some of the limits of social-movement politics, and even win elections, while maintaining much of the spirit of the squares. For others, municipalism is our first experience of political activism, allowing us to feel, for once, that we can have a say in the issues that affect us.

Our experience has taught us that the best way of showing that there is an alternative to the status quo is to start doing politics differently ourselves. The challenge is to do this without being either paralysed by the quest for democratic purity or disheartened by the inevitable limitations and contradictions that we will face along the way. Creating a winning municipalist candidacy is a constant balancing act, between consensus-seeking and the ability to make decisions and take action effectively; between promoting participation and preventing burnout; between horizontality and recognition of the role of leadership. When you find yourself facing down the political, economic and media establishment, it's important not to allow 'perfect' to be the enemy of 'good enough'. Deciding where to draw this line, on both a personal and a collective level, will be an ongoing dilemma throughout your journey.

In this chapter, we'll focus on building municipalist platforms with the goal of standing for local office, but it's important to remember that not all roads can, or should, lead to elections. Whether doing so makes sense for you will depend on the rules governing who can stand for election and how, on the electoral system, on the powers and resources of local government and on the strength of grassroots organizing in your town or city. It's worth bearing in mind that many of the municipal platforms that have won elections shortly after being set up emerged from social movements that were active for years, or even decades, previously. If you're starting from scratch, there's no need to rush; build your process so that each step serves to prove that your town or city could be run differently.

Mini-manifesto

- **Don't be afraid to take the lead.** We want to create a transparent, horizontal and democratic process but, ironically, someone has to take the lead and make sure this happens! Set up a pilot group to kick off the process and commit to democratizing the governance of the organization once it has been opened up and consolidated.

- **Ensure a gender balance and diversity from the start.** The pilot group must not be male-dominated; this is an essential element of the feminization of politics. It should reflect the ethnic and cultural diversity of your community, and include people with different skills, particularly in organizing, logistics and finance, communication and group facilitation.

- **Put shared goals at the centre.** The best place to begin is with how you want to change and improve your local area. Starting the process with your goals is the best way to engage people in the process, particularly people with no previous interest in electoral politics. Go out and ask people what they think about their neighbourhood, about how they would change it. Focusing on shared goals, rather than potentially divisive negotiations over who should stand as a candidate, is also a good way to bring people from diverse backgrounds and from different organizations together and to create a sense of common purpose.

- **Launch your platform publicly.** Set out some basic goals and values and invite people to join the process of construction. It's important to define the basic pillars of the project and leave margins for people to participate in building it from there.

- **Harness collective intelligence.** Invite people to contribute ideas about how to improve your neighbourhood, town or city, and debate how to make them a reality.

- **Hit the pavements and climb staircases.** The streets and squares are where relations happen and homes and backyards are where lives get reproduced. Be sure to take these spaces and the people in them seriously; value what they do to make city life possible. Don't limit your outreach to parties and social movements; make a particular effort to reach out to people who are politically disengaged and whose voices are not usually heard.

- **Communicate differently.** Use culture, music, art and memes to make politics fun. From tea (or wine!) gatherings at local community centres to posters and leaflets, to social media campaigns, go for what makes sense for you and don't feel you need to do everything. Speak and write like normal people, using everyday language and avoiding activist or ideological jargon. Draw on local geography, history and culture when choosing names, symbols and slogans for your platform (see Chapter 8).

- **Test popular support for a potential candidacy.** One way to legitimize the decision to stand in elections is to set a target of collecting a certain number of signatures of support for a statement of your goals and values (for example, one per cent of the city's population).

- **Decide who your candidate/s will be.** Don't hesitate to choose well-known, charismatic leaders, but ensure that there are mechanisms to hold them accountable. Consider holding open primaries, but be aware of the risks of stoking internal divisions. Try to encourage collaboration rather than competition in candidate selection processes, and to build teams that reflect the diversity of your movement.

Small victories and the politics of doing

Encouraging participation is easier said than done. In our experience, generating an action-oriented political culture is essential. Most people don't have lots of free time to spend in assemblies debating how to overthrow capitalism or drafting rules of procedure. They want to feel that the time they invest in any political process is useful; that they are making a contribution to transforming their communities. Base your platform on the politics of doing rather than of debating. Aim to find a role for everyone who wants to be involved, whether it be distributing flyers, fundraising or catering, and allow each working group or assembly to be relatively autonomous and test its ideas through processes of trial and error.

Action-based politics will help you to achieve small victories that show change is possible. Achieving concrete results, however limited, empowers people and encourages them to stay motivated and take on bigger challenges.

Examples

Let's Win Back Barcelona Manifesto, Barcelona

This is the statement that Barcelona En Comú (then called Let's Win Back Barcelona) issued in 2014, when it first decided to challenge the existing political system and put up candidates who would stand for election to the city council.

> Rescuing democracy from the powers that are holding it hostage is a difficult and ambitious, yet thrilling, challenge. It requires creating new tools for social and political action that connect organized citizens with those who are beginning to mobilize; people who have been campaigning for some time with those who feel cheated and are longing to get excited about a common project.
>
> That's why we are launching this citizen platform. To build a joint candidacy that represents the majority, with the aim to win. A candidacy that excites, that is based in neighbourhoods, workplaces, the cultural community, and that allows us to transform institutions for the benefit of the people.
>
> We don't want a coalition or an alphabet soup of political parties. We want to avoid the old logic of parties and build a new space that, while respecting the identity of everyone involved, is more than the sum of the parts that make it up. We believe that our city has what it takes to make this possible.

'People's Manifesto', Take Back the City, London

Take Back the City was set up by teachers and young people in London to challenge the mainstream 'business as usual' agenda in the 2015 city elections. They drew up a People's Manifesto by meeting with 75 different groups of people from across the city and asking 'What do you want from London? What does a fair/just London look like?' The process included online submissions, but the group prioritized in-person events, making a particular effort to reach out to marginalized groups such as office cleaners and people living in homeless shelters. They received about 2,000 submissions to the manifesto in total. The platform's activity was crowdfunded, with donations averaging £10.

Collecting signatures, Comú de Lleida
(Commons of Lleida), Lleida, Spain

Spanish law allows groups of local residents to stand for election without being members of a political party. Any group that collects a certain number of signatures of support (determined by the population of the municipality) can then run for office as a 'group of voters' (*agrupación de electores*) for one term. In 2015 the target in Lleida, a rural town with a population of 139,000, was 1,500 signatures in 20 days. A group of people with a background in social movements in the town drew up a manifesto committing to transparency, participation and the commons and managed to collect 2,000 signatures of support to stand as the group of voters 'Commons of Lleida'. The group went on to win two seats on the city council in the 2015 local elections.

Collaborative manifesto and election campaign,
Muitas pela Cidade que Queremos
(Many for the City We Want), Belo Horizonte, Brazil

In 2015 people from social movements in Belo Horizonte started to consider standing in the local elections and set up *Muitas*. From March to November the platform went out into parks, squares, schools and public spaces to collect ideas from residents about the issues they faced in the city, from pollution to mobility and urban violence. They drew up a 'Manifesto for the City We Want' based on the results of this process. The collective nature of the process gave it legitimacy and the text itself helped to communicate the platform's political identity.

The political party PSOL joined the process in 2016, giving *Muitas* the legal right to stand in the city elections. *Muitas* prioritized ethnic and gender diversity in its list of 12 candidates, which included the first indigenous and transsexual women candidates in the city's history.

Over 200 people participated in the platform's working groups during the October 2016 election campaign, including designers and artists who donated their work to raise funds. Local musicians composed jingles for each candidate, and 'biketivists' cycled around the city playing these through loudspeakers and flying flags with the faces of the candidates from their bikes. Less than two years after it was set up, *Muitas* received 35,000 votes and won two seats on the city council.

Open primaries, Movimiento Valparaíso Ciudadano (Citizen Movement of Valparaíso), Valparaíso, Chile

In 2016, an alliance of new national political parties, local political initiatives, social movements, the cultural sector, university students and professors, and small traders came together to create the Citizen Movement of Valparaíso. The movement held self-managed 'citizen primaries' to choose its mayoral candidate from among six people. The primary process, which saw ballot boxes placed in student associations, parks, shops, community centres and union offices, acted as an invitation to residents to actively engage in politics. In total, 5,200 people voted in the primaries, and the winner, Jorge Sharp, went on to be voted mayor in the October 2016 local elections.

Feminizing politics

Horizontal participation is one of the main ways of breaking down traditional structures of power and authority. But allowing open participation in a municipalist platform is not enough. We need to work actively to ensure that traditional power dynamics are not reproduced in our participatory processes. That means employing facilitation techniques that pay attention to gender parity and to the representation of other forms of diversity, for example, by limiting the length of people's speeches when they take the floor, and providing a range of mechanisms for people to contribute their ideas beyond public speaking (debates in small groups, writing on cards, digital participation, etc). It also means being aware of the extra time burden that political participation places on particular sectors of the population. This implies making participation processes short and time-efficient, providing on-site childcare, and varying the times meetings and assemblies are held.

How to participate in a municipalist assembly

Recommendations by Marea Feminista, the feminism group of municipalist platform Marea Atlántica (Atlantic Tide), A Coruña

1 When you arrive at the assembly, try to avoid sitting in the most important spot.

2 Even when you want to sit with people who are politically most like you, try to mix with people who are less politically similar to you too, particularly women.

3 When the debate is opened to the floor, don't be the first to speak, and remember there's nothing wrong with having a few minutes of reflection for those who have greater difficulty in expressing their ideas.

4 When you participate in a debate, consider whether what you are about to say has already been said by someone else and whether it's necessary to repeat it in order to add something. In this case, make reference to the person who already expressed the idea and add your contribution without repeating what's already been said.

5 Never try to translate, clarify or interpret what someone else has said, especially a woman. If you think something is unclear, ask her to explain it again or ask concrete questions about anything you find confusing.

6 When you're responding in a debate, try to space out your contributions.

7 Always try to bear in mind how many men and women are participating in the debate.

8 Try to estimate how long the interventions of other men and women in the group last and try to adjust your own to the average.

9 Consider your non-verbal communication, your physical position, and how you feel and gesticulate.

10 Moderate your tone of voice: shouting or being forceful shouldn't make an opinion count more.

Assemblies are spaces for the exchange of ideas in which everyone should be able to participate. Maybe you have all the answers, but if you don't leave space for others to contribute you'll monopolize the debate.

Facilitators are there for a reason; they make sure no-one sidetracks the debate, that all voices and perspectives can be heard before a decision is taken, and that we each see beyond our own perspective. This is their role and it should be respected.

Key concepts

Collective intelligence: This is about harnessing the knowledge, intelligence, wisdom, skill and ability of everyone in your community. Valuing collective intelligence will allow your platform to achieve things that seem impossible. Avoid concentrating authority and decision-making in single people or cliques of people, and build processes like open assemblies, workshops, surveys and brainstorming sessions to check in on, and further develop, your collective intelligence and practice. These processes will help you deal with expert knowledge, hierarchies and attacks by adversaries. Make sure you always draw on the knowledge of people affected by politics, not just on that of specialists or experts.

Tools and resources

Fearless Cities Workshop: 'How to create a participatory municipalist candidacy'
nin.tl/fearless

Let's Win Back Barcelona Manifesto
nin.tl/letswin

How to Win Back the City En Comú: guide to building a citizen municipal platform Barcelona En Comú
nin.tl/wincity

Now's the time to win A video explaining the process of building Barcelona En Comú
nin.tl/now

6

Code of ethics and financing

Xavi Ferrer (Barcelona En Comú), **Susi Capella** (València En Comú), **Pantxo Ramas** (Barcelona En Comú) and **Yolanda Sánchez** (Barcelona En Comú)

It's only by avoiding getting into debt with the banks that we can say and do what we really believe to be for the best.
Miguel Ongil, Podemos Madrid

A code of ethics is not a way to make oneself immune to corruption, but is rather the mechanism by which, when someone acts in an incorrect way, he or she can be removed from their duties.
Ximo Balaguer, Barcelona En Comú

Context

The current lack of legitimacy in the political system is to a large extent due to corruption and the links between major political parties and the large economic powers. The revolving door between elected office and corporations, secret meetings, personal gifts, family dynasties in public office, bribes, theft and bank loans to finance election campaigns: all these and more have led to a complete lack of confidence in institutional politics.

In this context, politicians must make a new pact with the people. The new pact should bring with it a new set of rules which go further than a vague commitment to 'good governance' and which instead create a new political ethics, aimed at radical democratization of both politics and the economy.

Because of this, many political candidacies are incorporating into their programme a new contract between the public and people elected to public office. This includes new forms of financing which allow parties to maintain their independence from banks. This new code of ethics is key at the municipal level, where the contact between political representatives and the people is much closer, and where participation is vital in order to create a democratic society. Municipalism allows us to use this closeness to create a new code of ethics and also to develop new forms of financing that are transparent and independent from the banks.

Mini-manifesto

How to draw up a code of ethics

- **A code of ethics should be useful to its organization** in order to:
    - democratize decision-making and internal responsibility;
    - promote collaborative financing – financing that receives resources from a wide base so as to be free of banks and so-called 'major donors';
    - obtain financial information and statements of ethical principles from partner organizations;
    - eliminate privilege and prevent corruption;
    - ensure an open and coherent process for the election of technical workers and people in sensitive positions.
- **It must be demanding** but also realistic, and allow organizations to function. A good code of ethics will show society the organization's commitment to political ethics in a real, implementable and practical way.
- **It must be binding** for all members and collaborators of the political organization; we must all agree to it.
- **It must be reviewable.** The organization must be ready to reconsider how to fulfil its promises and be prepared to change the way it acts if necessary.
- **It must be concrete.** The code must be subject to regulation, with imprecise rules avoided and simple mechanisms to measure compliance.
- **It must be comprehensible.** A code of ethics is a tool used to build a healthy organization, and so it must be easy to

understand both within the organization and outside it.
- **Assemblies and working groups are necessary** to define the principal points of a code of ethics.
- The following three points are recommended when creating of a code of ethics:
  - **Building consensus** around certain principles, involving all the individuals who will participate in the candidacy;
  - **Creating a draft** of the code of ethics as well as the tools for changing it before a final vote;
  - **Putting in place a protocol** to modify the code when changes are necessary, and to define which body will make sure the code is adhered to.

The following elements must be combined in a coherent way in the code of ethics:
- upper limits to salaries;
- ways of avoiding the creation of political elites who make a living from politics rather than using it to serve the people;
- mechanisms to increase women's participation in politics;
- criteria by which to stop dependency on the banks and other organizations;
- term limits;
- ways to avoid conflicts of interest when politicians are in office and also when they leave it;
- guarantees of transparency in political activity.

How to raise money

Another important step when a municipalist platform is preparing a political campaign is fundraising.

1 Political campaigns are more expensive than many groups can afford, yet at the same time have to be carried out with great transparency. Two factors in any success are creativity and a willingness to ask for money. The key is to think that financing a political party is not something purely monetary, but also a political tool.

2 One needs to be efficient and able to reach possible donors (activists or supporters), and in order to bring in donations it is essential to be flexible and define different fundraising

actions for different goals, audiences and funding channels. It is vital to keep the digital divide in mind, as not everyone uses the internet in the same way or to the same extent.

3 The most important thing is to gain people's trust: one must be real, transparent and supportive, and not simply appear so. Money should not be a barrier to collaborating with a particular group, but rather a way of showing that you have faith in the project, and so individuals should not be persuaded to donate because, for example, it's not a great effort to do so, but rather because it is a worthwhile thing to do: to donate money in a focused and resolute way is a transformative political act. Political finance is political activism and a way of joining the movement that we love.

4 In order for the call for funds to be successful, the whole organization must be mobilized: one's neighbours, one's family and oneself must be convinced that collective financing is desirable and necessary.

Fundraising tools

Crowdfunding. Small sums; lots of donors; emotional decision to invest. Anyone can do it!

Personal microcredit. Larger sums; formal contracts used. The source for this is people who might or might not be involved in the political project, but who know and trust people who are involved (relatives, friends etc).

Merchandising. This normally becomes more an element of marketing than an important way of gathering funds. It is usually directed mainly at activists themselves – unless there is a large-scale marketing campaign under way – and it is more important that people wear our T-shirt in public than that they give us money for it.

Regular contributions. It is useful to maintain a wide donor base in order to cover fixed structural costs. Crowdfunding and microcredit can also be used to finance specific projects and campaigns.

Other. Periodic or individual donations, electoral grants, donations in kind.

Examples

Crowdfunding, Barcelona En Comú, Barcelona

From the start, fundraising was a major challenge. We considered a large number of options, but at first we couldn't decide how or when to get started. In retrospect, it became clear that it was the group itself that did not feel comfortable with fundraising.

We had to get over our fears and create a wave of joy around the fundraising project. We did this by using the idea of 'what you can't do on your own becomes possible with the help of your friends', which we began to explain to as many people as possible. We took part in all the meetings held by Barcelona En Comú in order to explain the importance of the crowdfunding campaign; we organized meetings at all public events; we went round all the local groups, in order to co-ordinate the sale of merchandise; and we carried out publicity campaigns to promote the microcredit model, explaining the technical details to everyone who asked: 'A maximum of 10,000 euros, payment in a year, no interest...' It sounded like a broken record, but this was the key to our success.

Our donations ended up at more than 90,000 euros; there were more than 200 microcredit loans, and hundreds of people were brought in to participate in the campaign. It became very clear that the ethics of the organization were not simply a code of behaviour, but rather a live and shared adventure, made up of people, decisions, doubts, choices and mistakes; converting all this into collective effort is what gave a new ethical focus to Barcelona En Comú.

Donations and reimbursable bonds, Valencia En Comú, Valencia

In order to finance its campaign for the 2015 municipal elections, Valencia En Comú launched a set of **donations and reimbursable bonds** aimed at politicizing fundraising and making it more democratic.

They did this with three clear objectives. First of all, they aimed to preserve their independence and not have recourse to a bank in order to obtain funding: they preferred to go into debt with the citizenry rather than with some bank. Second, they undertook to identify anyone who bought a bond. This was a requirement demanded by the ministry in order to comply with the funding laws for political parties, but they transformed it into a mechanism for increased transparency, in order to say publicly – and not just to the Finance Ministry – who had funded the platform. Third, this was a way to break down the digital divide and give a chance to those people who did not have access to the internet or who were not savvy with new technologies the opportunity to make donations to the cause, whether by buying donation bonds, or else granting mini-credits to the organization via reimbursable bonds.

Some 56 per cent of the campaign's income came from these bonds, which allowed the organization to put together a street-level, more direct campaign, not just as a result of the 10,000 euros which the campaign gathered, but also because the local sales in the streets became a key part of the campaign itself, because it was Valencia En Comú which approached people in order to ask for a donation or a microcredit loan, and was therefore able to explain the political project to them at the same time. They were able to show that it was not just with words but also with actions that they were creating a new kind of politics, one that was closer to the citizenry, as well as participative, open and neighbourhood-based.

Code of ethics, Marea Atlántica, A Coruña

Given the need to create a new sense of legitimacy in a political environment filled with cases of corruption and influence-peddling, the citizen platform Marea Atlántica decided to start a debate to see what demands and areas of mistrust people on the street might have towards a new political project.

In the process very many ideas were gathered and grouped into a format which was internally consistent and cohesive: this was designed to be understandable to a general audience, and for the ethical decisions taken to be clear and public. And this was how Marea Atlántica's code of ethics was written.

It was published in a simple and approachable format, the text dotted with hashtags and images, and, although it is always difficult to judge the impact of initiatives like this, it did generate a great deal of media coverage and was one of the most visited parts of the organization's website during the campaign. Elements of it, such as the #UnaPersonaUnCargo (#OnePersonOneJob) hashtag, the capping of salaries or #Transparencia were topics that were discussed during the campaign, in the media as well as in the street. And so, the process and the results we obtained opened up a new political space where, beyond what was required by law, a stronger commitment to democratic values was generated.

'Piggy Bank', Badalona En Comú, Badalona

As a result of the self-imposed cap on salaries, one of the rules of the code of ethics, there was a difference between the maximum salary available (3.5 times the minimum salary for this particular profession) and the amounts paid to the elected members of Badalona En Comú by the local government.

This sum was known as 'excess salary' and every public official in Badalona En Comú paid by the City Council had to put it into the platform's shared 'piggy bank'. In order to put this excess money to good use, it was dedicated to social projects, chosen by participants in the 'Pot Comú' campaign; in the first year 30,000 euros were donated to charitable causes.

Feminizing politics

Any code of ethics code needs to include methods for transforming and feminizing politics, and to acknowledge how difficult it is for women to participate in a world whose procedures, working hours, and dynamics of relationship and public appearance are all profoundly masculine. The key to introducing feminist principles into political action is to make politics more human, more horizontal and more collective. To create a new ethics regarding the link between citizen representation and citizens themselves is one way of opening up the debate on participation, representation and transparency, but it will also help us to think about work-life balance and how we intend to combine our productive work with our reproductive care. At the same time, to insist on financing our actions in a collaborative and decentralized way is a way to take a collective decision with greater autonomy and in a more personally direct fashion. Relationships based on trust and confidence are vital to this.

Key concepts

Code of ethics: the chief aim of this is to eliminate the current level of privilege among those who wish to dedicate themselves to politics, by placing caps on salaries, making agendas public, removing bonuses, making it impossible for politicians to move into lucrative 'advisory' jobs after they leave office, and so on. This is an 'ethical contract' between people who occupy public office and the public.

Crowdfunding: a citizens' campaign, popular and decentralized, set up in order to generate funds and promote participation in and commitment to the political project. It attempts to be viral, to travel by word of mouth, and to democratize the way in which funds are gathered. Its aim is collective empowerment and it does not depend on any one individual, because it is preferable to have a large number of individuals giving a small amount each than to have a small number making large donations.

Tools and resources

Fearless Cities roundtable: 'Code of ethics and party funding'
nin.tl/ethics

The code of ethics of Barcelona En Comú
nin.tl/code

7

Organizing a municipalist platform: structure and confluence

Marta Junqué (Barcelona En Comú), **Caren Tepp** (City Councillor from Rosario, Argentina) and **Mariano Fernández** (Marea Atlántica)

The vital thing is how to make people who come to our organization feel that they are transforming reality.

Caren Tepp, Ciudad Futura

Context

Municipalism is a movement that aims to go beyond changing public policy or sending 'better' people to pre-existing institutions: it also wants to change how politics is done, to take back the city, and to use the strength of the people to put local institutions at the service of the common good. It is not enough for us to have a good manifesto or leaders who are clever and committed. We want to be protagonists of a collective project, which is why building a municipalist organization is essential, both at the start of the process and once the project has been consolidated. Our organizations have to be a reflection of the transformative politics we defend: they have to promote internal democracy, the feminization of politics, working as a network and a collective intelligence.

We are aware that each local context is different, that each local area has its own traditions, its own political culture,

49

organizations, movements and parties, and each organization needs to find the structure most useful to its project. There are no hard and fast rules about how a municipalist platform should be structured, but there has been a great deal of thought given to it in different places and different circumstances. Here we will explore the organizational characteristics shared by most municipalist platforms.

Mini-manifesto

A 'confluence' is more than a mere 'coalition' of parties. How can we create confluence?

A municipalist organization must ensure that everyone can participate on an equal footing, especially those people who have no previous experience of electoral politics. The challenge is to create an organization that includes and is based on the experience of previous movements and political parties, but which is more than the sum of its parts. The central element of this process is confluence.

- **Increase citizen participation.** When we launch our platform we must be capable of reaching out to citizens who are not members of existing parties and movements and inspire them to get to know and participate in the activities of this new organization.
- **Goals are more important than labels.** Confluence means building relationships with different actors: not just political parties, but also local people and social movements – anyone who shares our aims and strategies for action can contribute to the movement.
- **Working together on concrete goals and projects**. We have to develop processes that allow us to identify the concrete goals and actions at municipal level that will allow different people and organizations to work together.
- **Promote citizen leadership.** It is important for new faces to be seen on the political stage, and for a wide consensus to be established among all the members of a platform. Efforts must be made to identify and bring into the project people who can contribute to its development and implementation with a variety of different skill sets and

from a variety of different backgrounds (political, technical, communications, public relations, etc).

- **Individual participation.** A fundamental requirement for radical democracy and the feminization of politics is for people to participate in the organization as individuals (independent of their role in the party organs, its institutions, or society in general). There should be no quotas relating to the representation of organizations or parties within the municipalist platform.
- **Generosity as a key value.** True confluence requires high levels of individual generosity in support of the common project and the concrete objectives to be achieved. It is equally important to value activists with previous experience as it is to value the fresh perspectives brought by people who are participating in politics for the first time.
- **Promote permeability and 'double function' among activists.** Managing the relationship between the municipalist platform and those organizations and parties that are also active at other levels of government is one of the most complicated parts of the process. It is important that the platform be permeable to the demands of social movements and open to activist participation. The presence of activists who are members of two, three or four organizations is desirable but complex to manage.

How do we structure the platform to respond to democratic radicalism and the feminization of politics?

- **We need bodies that take collective decisions and that can break up the old vertical dynamics, guarantee gender parity, and promote collective leadership.** When the structure of the organization is decided, a few things must be incorporated: multiple political posts held by a single individual should be avoided; gender parity (a minimum of 50-per-cent women) must be observed; and measures must be put into place to facilitate collective decision-making.
- **Local neighbourhood assemblies have to be well represented** in the organizational model, and in a living, dynamic way. Municipalism's force comes from local

assemblies and small-scale local organizations. The work of local activists is a vital bridge between the organization and other local movements, as well as grounding the organization in the daily life of its environment and making sure it is constantly aware of the realities within which it lives.

- **There should be organizational flexibility and a capacity to adapt to the needs of each context.** The organizational model needs to be able to adapt to each specific context, and to the needs of each phase of the organization; it also needs to be able to learn from its mistakes. It has to be something that is living and flexible, but it also needs some core areas (for work, participation and decision-making) that are stable enough to help foster an organizational culture based on values and principles. The technical team needs to work in accordance with the organization's structure and internal dynamics.

- **There must be collaboration and permeability between elected council members and the organization as a whole.** It is not easy to maintain an organization that is active and permeable at the same time as governing. If the platform is running the municipal government, it is vital to keep alive the institutional space (formed by the mayor, the councillors, district councillors, etc) as part of the platform itself. Various dynamics (reflection and mutual decision-making, to name just two) need to be supported in order to make sure that these two areas are permeable and share strategies that relate to their goals and ways of working.

- **Create different spaces for participation and decision-making.** Decisions should be the result of debate and voting via easily understandable mechanisms. In order to be consistent with the principles of internal democracy, all participation processes should be based on collective intelligence and working as a network.

- **Create roles and tasks appropriate for all levels of involvement so as to maximize inclusion.** In order to make sure that the organization flourishes, participation has to be flexible and move beyond the idea of only allowing a say to participants who attend meetings in person: instead, it must promote care, work-life balance and diversity when it comes to dividing up time and tasks.

- **Do not suppress conflict.** Internal criticism and a diversity of opinions will make the organization grow. Conflict should be seen as a revitalizing force and we should seek consensus through honest and open debate. We should use debates to reduce the distances between differing positions and find solutions, rather than taking decisions based on small majorities in a way that creates 'winners' and 'losers'.

Examples

An organizational model based on internal democracy, working as a network and promoting collective intelligence: Barcelona En Comú, Barcelona

The structure of Barcelona En Comú is made up of different areas of participations in which decisions are taken, space for reflection is provided and working groups are set up. The most important participatory spaces are:

- **The Comú**, which is made up of about 15,000 registered supporters, who do not participate in any of its formal work spaces. The Comú holds the project to account and helps make political and organizational decisions. The members participate via an online platform.
- **The Plenary**, which takes most strategic decisions and which is open to all activists who participate in one of the platform's working groups or local assemblies. It is currently made up of around 1,500 people.
- **The Co-ordination Assembly**, which is made up of people selected from different participation areas and is responsible for establishing the political strategy of the organization. It includes four members of the municipal government.
- **The Executive**, which is made up of a small number of members elected by activists; it takes operational decisions and carries out the strategies formulated by the Co-ordination Assembly.

- **Neighbourhood assemblies**, made up of activists from each neighbourhood; these need to be self-managed and have operational autonomy. All neighbourhood assemblies meet in the territorial co-ordination assembly.
- **The Policy Groups**, made up of activists with experience of or interest in a particular sectoral theme. Every two weeks these different groups meet to co-ordinate and work on reports in the policy co-ordination assembly.
- **The Guarantee Committee**, which is an independent body made up of members elected by activists. This is responsible for ensuring the democratic functioning of the platform and guaranteeing the application of the principles of equal participation, fairness and transparency.

Evolution of an organizational model: Marea Atlántica, A Coruña

Marea Atlántica was born in the summer of 2014. Its structure combines the principle of democratic innovation with the most obvious organizational needs: empowerment, territorial extension and discourse. In order to effect this, Marea is divided into three fundamental organs: the *Rede*, which is the deliberative grouping, formed as a plenary and authorized to take strategic decisions; the *Apertura*, an executive body in charge of political relations; and the *Co-ordinating Body*, which runs Marea Atlántica's day-to-day business. There are also working groups (both sectoral and territorial) but these do not have specific competencies.

In May 2015, Marea Atlántica won the local elections. Since its accession to power, the work of government has moved extremely rapidly – much more rapidly than the working groups of Marea itself, which is something that has provoked frustration among these groups. In order to sort out this organizational inefficiency, a new methodology and means of organization was trialled in 2017, clarifying what the working groups' functions were. It assigned them the role of building alliances to strengthen public policy, working more on concrete projects rather than on broad thematic areas, and, above all, opening up their work so as to allow people not officially connected to the organization to take part. As an example of how these new structures work, one of their current projects is to study the wildfires of 2017. The working group doing this is made up of people from different sectors and areas, as well as people who are not official activists of the organization.

This organizational adaptation, approved in the 2018 plenary, has clarified the way in which political initiatives that derive from the working groups can be implemented, as well as the functions of the groups themselves. The adaptation has also helped to test the four key documents of the group (code of ethics, structure, governance and elections to the leadership) and to formalize the idea that these four documents should be revised every two years.

The three organizational driving forces of Ciudad Futura, Rosario, Argentina

Ciudad Futura came into being at the end of 2012 when two of the most highly developed social movements in the Argentinian city of Rosario came together. These movements had almost a decade of independent local activism behind them before the agreement was reached to found Ciudad Futura as a movement party: a political instrument that would support the expansion of social movements (concentrating on community organization and non-state bodies in working-class areas of the city), both locally and by occupying the municipal government. Ciudad Futura managed to get four candidates elected to the city's legislative assembly.

The organizational structure of Ciudad Futura has changed over time, using the organization's experience to adapt and to strengthen the process of political expansion and consolidation. Ciudad Futura has recently codified its three organizational driving forces, its 'motors', which are designed to work in a linked yet autonomous fashion on a single political strategy based on collective wisdom.

Motor 1: Autonomy. This gathers together all the 'strategic projects' of Ciudad Futura (managed by non-state and co-operative institutions): these include the two public and socially managed secondary schools, the Practical University and the 'Misión Anti Inflación' collaborative consumer network.

Motor 2: Local organization. This is a way of organizing local activists, who are divided into groups according to their city sector (sectors are the smallest administrative districts of the city, sometimes overlapping city districts), as well as allocated to six District Centres.

Motor 3: Government. This consists of the four councillors and their legislative team (everyone on the team is paid the same salary, and most of their governmental earnings are paid into a fund that guarantees the financial autonomy of the organization).

To these three 'motors' can be added: the 'executive assembly', made up of the co-ordinators of the groups inside each of the three 'motors'; the 'members' assembly', made up of anyone who is an active participant in any of the groupings within any of the three 'motors'; and the 'citizens' assembly', which was conceived as an open space for dialogue with the public in order to start political conversations on the current situation and to gather collective wisdom.

Feminizing politics

The struggle to feminize our organizations is a permanent one. We always try to do what we can, and assign some of our financial resources to help alleviate particular problems, such as that of providing childcare at meetings, but these actions are clearly insufficient. Men and women are given equal positions in the key organizations, but this isn't a perfect solution either. The feminization (or perhaps it is better to call it the de-patriarchalization) of politics needs to become a part of the structure of all political organizations and their actions. In order to make sure this happens, we cannot ignore the relationship between masculinity and power, so important in the way men construct their identities as well as in the socialization of women.

It is therefore important to open up spaces that deconstruct male power and empower women. In addition, we need to develop methods to show where the discrepancies are to be found, to deal with areas of conflict and to come down hard on possible cases and situations of abuse. As well as this, time management is key, and all participative processes need to be planned well in advance, with consideration given to the areas in which they take place, their formal aspects, and their methodology (women and men should be given equal time and space to speak, and the tone and length of their participation should be managed). One final point: it is, clearly, difficult to take on all this with a focus on sustainability and care. Institutional and activist environments are not usually sustainable, and need active strategies and programmes (such as financial aid, family-friendly organization of events, timetable changes and so on) to make sure that they are welcoming to women.

Key concepts

Confluence: For all municipalist platforms, confluence is the central element of the organizational process. This refers to alliances between related political projects (parties, movements, citizens' platforms and individuals), which try to move beyond the logic of traditional coalitions. Rather than using quotas to represent different organizations, or trying to keep them separate from one another, a confluence is based on bringing people together to participate as individuals, whatever their affiliation with other political projects.

Tools and resources

Fearless Cities roundtable: 'Organizing a municipalist platform: structure and confluence'
nin.tl/workshop6

Organizational structure of Barcelona En Comú
This document explains the organizational model which the platform put in place after winning the municipal elections (the so-called Phase D):
nin.tl/BEC

There's 30,000 of us, and more to come! A video that explains the values of Barcelona En Comú.
nin.tl/BECvalues

Casting Shadows: Chokwe Lumumba and the struggle for racial justice and economic democracy in Jackson, Mississippi
Kali Akuno, 2015. This book explains how local organizations managed to combine and raise their struggle to the national level, taking the election of Patrice Lumumba as their model.
nin.tl/rosalux

8

Communication for municipalist transformation

Adrià Rodríguez (Barcelona En Comú) and **Alejandra Calvo** (Ahora Madrid)

The 1-9-90 rule suggests that in any social media campaign, 1 per cent of the people will create content, 9 per cent will be active sharers and editors of the content, and 90 per cent will only consume the content. Our aim is to gain the support of the 9 per cent.

Emma Avilés, 15M activist

The feedback between the street and the internet, the physical layer and the digital layer, reorganizes power in such a way that when we occupy all the places available, the mainstream media will have to talk about us and work within structures we dictate.

Javier Toret, 15M activist

Context

All communication is political, as it transforms to a certain extent our relations with others and with the world. Communication plays a key role in any transformative project, and municipalism is no exception. What is more, political communication at a local level is an extremely potent tool. We are living through a period in which trust in traditional parties is very low, communications channels are saturated, and ideologies are ever more polarized. We no longer believe in electoral promises; we no longer trust the mass media. We often refuse to listen to those who think differently from us, and we huddle down alongside 'our' people, especially online, where we live in our social bubbles.

Municipalist communication helps us to break down these dynamics thanks to working at a smaller, local scale. This kind of communication – listening to others and explaining ourselves to them – is not at all like appearing on a television talk show or writing a newspaper column.

The local scale allows us to harness communication to identify shared goals, despite our differences, to generate a 'common sense' at the neighbourhood or city level, and to come together to win. Even when we do not manage to achieve our objectives or involve more people, the local scale humanizes us; it helps us to understand one another better and communicate in a more feminized way.

Political communication is key to our municipalist plans for the future. This is the case for various reasons. First of all, it allows us to shift public opinion during election campaigns. Second, it is only through creativity and imagination that we are able to expand the limits of the possible within any institution. Third, communication allows us to establish links between institutions and the political movements that feed into them. Finally, municipalist communication is a powerful weapon in the fight against the far right, as it allows us to generate local collective identities that are not reliant on markers of ethnicity or citizenship. Shared stories, music and images can generate a sense of belonging in our districts and cities, and make us see ourselves in our neighbours, wherever they may have come from.

In order to achieve this it was vital, in our case, to go beyond traditional politics and use the technopolitical innovations that movements such as the Arab Spring, 15M, Occupy, Occupy Gezi and YoSoy132 adopted with such success. We are currently trying to make use of technopolitical methods to win over our cities and put them at the service of the common good.

Mini-manifesto

- **Avoid sectarian language**, which is often rooted in the traditional Left or the activist community. The goal is to bring in people from diverse backgrounds, including people who are not politicized, and to eventually become a majority.
- **Use familiar and comprehensible language**, referring to concrete things (air quality, high rents, etc) instead of abstract or theoretical concepts.
- **Bring different media spaces into play.** Communicate through different media spaces at the same time, including social media and tools of mass communication. It is important to promote connection and feedback between different media.
- **Look for language and symbols that are widely known and shared**, especially those that are connected to geography, history and local identity, such as the notion of the *marea* ('tide'), which movements in coastal cities have adopted.
- **Be rigorous.** Send out and share information that is precise and truthful. Credibility is fundamental if the information we wish to transmit is to be widely shared.
- **It is not enough to be right** or to transmit information: we need to communicate from the heart in order to connect to and communicate with the city.
- **Think 'Yes We Can'.** We need to communicate in a way that is empowering, porous, open and joyful, that transmits the happiness we feel when transforming our shared reality. Use humour and irony as often as possible. It is the right wing that uses hatred and fear, but laughter is a key element in the language of social transformation.
- **Communicate for confluence.** We should create new symbols and inclusive collective identities that everyone is comfortable with, but which also appeal beyond the backgrounds and traditions that make up our platform.
- **Promote 'guerrilla' formats and actions** that can be used to empower people to appropriate and play with communications media, and which promote remix culture, the mixing of various worldviews and the use of memes. We

will only be able to communicate for municipalist change if we go viral, if people take on our message, our language, our story and our tools, and make them their own.

- **Be a swarm.** Promote decentralized, networked communication and focus all nodes of the network on the same goal in order to achieve it; the more people who communicate in a synchronized fashion, the further the message will travel and the greater the impact it will have. This is why we use digital tools which allow us to create and share collaborative content in a decentralized way.
- **Don't confuse communication with political participation.** Digital tools blur the boundaries of traditional political organizations and widen the ways in which we can participate in politics. To participate in communication means participating in a common narrative. But communication cannot be a substitute for or be understood as other forms of formal political participation: meetings, assemblies and so on. Communication tools can increase the number of ways in which we participate in the political process, but it is important not to limit participation to this alone.
- **Don't confuse communication with the organization that communicates.** Communication is key to building an organization and spreading its narrative (organizing meetings, or grouping the community round a single concrete objective, for example), but it cannot replace the organization itself.

Examples

The Duck, Ne de(vi)mo Beograd, Belgrade

On 2 April 2015, the duck appeared for the first time in front of the Parliament building in Belgrade, just when local government officials were voting to approve a *lex specialis*, a law deliberately written to help the investor behind the Belgrade Waterfront urban redevelopment project. In Serbian, 'duck' is a slang term for 'scam' or 'con'. In a few weeks, with the help of 2,000 demonstrators, it became clear that the Belgrade Waterfront project was exactly that, a scam, a clear case of urban speculation that would end up increasing the public debt and privatizing 1.8 square kilometres of the banks of the Sava.

After the elections of 24 April 2016, the duck appeared once again, in front of the Parliament building, wearing a painted mask. The police took the mask and sent it to the city dump. But this was not the end of the duck, who appeared more and more often, and in different forms: at demonstrations, in caricatures, in Facebook profile pictures, in illustrations, in homemade posters inviting people to local assemblies, in placards and on T-shirts. Little by little, it made it into the mainstream media, who started to criticize urban development in Belgrade.

The duck became such a powerful icon that it made sure that people didn't forget about Ne da(vi)mo Beograd, the initiative behind it, not even when the organization decided to call off the demonstrations and plan how to present itself at the local elections. The duck was a clear and humorous focal point for the hard work of activists and citizens. It became the symbol of the resistance and the catalyst for citizen participation.

In March 2018, Ne da(vi)mo Beograd stood for the first time in the municipal elections. During the campaign, a car that had been mocked up to look like a duck, the so-called 'duck-mobile', drove round the city to all the points at which aggressive and speculative building work was taking place, encouraging people to decide for themselves about the fates of their districts and their city as a whole.

Newspaper of the Future, La Capital 2021, Ciudad Futura, Rosario

Newspaper of the Future was an intervention designed by Ciudad Futura in the last week of the municipal election campaign in Rosario, Argentina, in 2017. The material that was produced was a mock-up of *La Capital*, the newspaper with the widest circulation in the city, which contained news reports of events taking place in 2021. The idea was to show how the city would change if the ideas promoted by Ciudad Futura were accepted and how they could change the city and its daily life, and introduce a new way of doing politics to the people of Rosario. The format of the paper was identical to that of *La Capital*, and so the citizens of Rosario were encouraged to think that the large changes that were required were not impossible and might even be closer than expected… Some 80,000 copies of the fake newspaper were designed, printed and distributed to people's houses, and to various distribution points around the city. Copies were also left in public institutions and popular spots in Rosario.

Digital media and public presence, Zaragoza en Común, Zaragoza

During Zaragoza en Común's election campaign, their communications strategy was based on the possibilities offered by digital media and a desire to be intensively present in the public space.

Using digital media (social networks, the web, instant messaging services) was not easy. On the one hand, the fact that the movement had changed its name meant that its Facebook account needed to be closed and restarted. On the other hand, a large number of the candidates did not have any previous public profiles on social media, and the top candidate on the movement's list, Pedro Santisteve, had no digital presence at all. But even taking these difficulties into account, the number of followers multiplied quickly and soon there were far more of them than for any other political grouping on Zaragoza City Council. This was the first sign that 'something was working'.

The other part of the strategy consisted in developing an intense and widely dispersed presence in the whole of the city's public space. Throughout the campaign there was a marquee in the Plaza del Pilar, the historic centre of the city, and this served as the central hub for the movement, a place where people could meet and where large numbers of activities were organized: speeches, games, debates, concerts, performances, meetings and so on. Also, instead of arranging a single large meeting to gather all their forces in one spot, it was decided to have smaller meetings in every district of the city, in the street, with the candidates for the particular district appearing alongside significant figures from each particular locality (activists, members of neighbourhood associations, artists): this allowed them to get through to a large portion of the population.

Guerrilla communication, the Barcelona and Madrid Graphic Liberation Movements

A group of illustrators, artists and designers became involved in the municipal election campaign with one objective: to spread the word and have people appropriate and make their own the set of ideas connected with Ada Colau (Barcelona) and Manuela Carmena (Madrid), to help them win the elections. The Barcelona and Madrid Graphic Liberation Movements were formed of individuals who were directly involved with the municipal candidacies while co-ordinating a large number of other people who collaborated on specific projects. This was how they managed to create a large number of images and illustrations, and how they also got creative professionals throughout the city to feel involved and implicated in this municipalist battle. The Barcelona and Madrid Graphic Liberation Movements are examples of how we can carry out guerrilla communications, with projects that are completely open to anyone who cares to join in, and which harness the twin powers of the street and the internet, bringing in the creative and the professional sectors in order to create winning imagery.

Feminizing politics

When it comes to political communication, there is one myth which dominates all messages, particularly their form: the myth of the superman. This superman embraces all possible topics and is able to articulate his view on them without any hesitation or doubt, usually displaying his strength and daring. If there are powerful communicators in the movement, then they need to be used and used well, but the main aim should be to abandon the idea of the supreme leader and move instead to that of collective leadership.

In order to subvert the idea of the superhero, we need to:

- make constant reference to the work that the various outreach teams are doing; show how joyous this local work can be; gather the sense of a powerful movement that comes from all the people who join the campaign freely;
- create different visible media figures and spokespeople;
- make the web of relationships visible, show the inter-dependence of any one group with those other movements that they walk alongside and whose achievements are worthy of grateful support.

In addition, an important aspect of the de-patriarchalization of communications media, and the politics that it derives from, has to be the abandonment of warlike messages that are aggressive, doctrinaire and closed to argument. In opposition to these messages, language must be developed that emphasizes mutual care and human closeness, that connects with people emotionally and acknowledges their daily struggles, and that tackles opponents with humour, sarcasm, and the security that comes from feeling together and united, rather than superior.

Key concepts

Technopolitics: the tactical and strategic use of the web and collective identities to connect brains and bodies in order to communicate, organize and act. This is not simple 'clicktivism': the corrupt old system is not going to change because of Facebook 'likes' or a petition on Change.org. Neither is it 'cyberactivism', which deals only with the digital realm. Technopolitics seeks to hack the mainstream and subject it to so much stress that people go onto the streets; it also relies on the idea of a feedback loop between the digital and the physical realms.

Tools and resources

Fearless Cities roundtable: 'Social Networks'
nin.tl/roundtable

And Then We Won the Election: The Book   This book describes the Movimiento de Liberación Gráfica (Graphic Liberation Movement). It gathers together the BGLM and MGLM illustrations from the municipal campaign of 2015.

9

Municipalism in small towns and rural areas

Jean Boulton (Independents for Frome), **Mercè Amich Vidal** (Councillor for Youth and Equality, Celrà City Council) and **Laura Bergés** (El Comú de Lleida)

In the context of austerity, people in small towns have two choices: we can either do without services or we can band together and organize and find a way of doing it for ourselves.

Pamela Barrett, Mayor of Buckfastleigh

When you try to implement transformative policies in a small town you have to stand up to entrenched interests, and these aren't the directors of multinationals, rather they're probably your friend's father, your own grandfather, and the owner of the corner shop where you buy your soap.

Mercè Amich Vidal,
Councillor for Youth and Equality, Celrà City Council

Context

Municipalism is often misunderstood as being about the politics of cities or of urban issues. In fact, municipalism, as a locally based, participatory way of doing politics, can be practised anywhere, from the largest city to the smallest village. While we can recognize that cities are a particularly relevant site of political action, we must also be wary of an urban discourse with which many banks, investment funds and traders are comfortable. The municipalist movement values cities as smaller units of government that are close to the people, for their capacity to harness diversity and generate new collective identities, and for their potential to reduce carbon emissions, not as investment havens or sources of cheap, precarious labour.

And however important cities are, it's important to remember that a third of the world's urban population lives in small or medium-sized towns, and that 45 per cent of the global population lives in rural areas. Any transformative movement must be open and useful to people in small towns and rural areas. Indeed, in many countries around the world we have seen the far right take hold in such areas, where people have often felt abandoned by national politicians and have been offered no positive alternative.

Indeed, in many ways, municipalism is easier and more effective in small towns than in large cities. To start with, building a municipalist platform in a small community where direct contact with most residents is possible involves lower communication costs and simpler organizational models. The relatively low barriers to entry to the lowest level of government in small towns has allowed new initiatives to flourish in many countries over recent years. In the UK, for example, the 'indy towns' movement has seen groups of independent candidates, tired of partisan battles, stand for local office and fight back against austerity. Such movements allow people of different political persuasions, ages and interests to work together to make their town or region thrive. They can tackle the particular challenges that exist locally, making the most of the complex and quirky local mix of skills, talents, assets, geography, culture and commerce.

Municipalist movements in small towns and rural areas also have advantages once in office. To begin with, the feeling of belonging in small towns often makes it easier to create a sense of community and common purpose to drive political action and agree on what needs to be done. In addition, the smaller the community, the more direct the lines of dialogue between residents and their local councils can be; this allows local councillors to get a direct and broad-ranging perspective on the needs and priorities of the community and to develop solutions in response. Smaller populations also offer greater potential to directly involve people both in decision-making processes and in making things happen, and there's a much greater opportunity in small towns to implement measures that have a direct impact. In this context, participative, independent politics, focused on local agendas and bringing together local resources to tackle local issues, is gaining traction and leading to success, as measured by economic vibrancy (and a growth in independent businesses), a reduction in inequality and the enhancement of a 'can do', innovative culture.

Of course, there are challenges too: in many countries centralization trends have reduced the legal powers of the 'lowest' levels of local government, or eliminated this level of government completely and replaced it with larger, regional institutions. Local councils often do not control transport infrastructure or social care, education or health budgets. Even on the issues where municipalities do have legal powers (such as urban planning), they often have limited resources and tax-raising powers to fund significant change. Rural areas often face particular problems, such as youth exodus and shrinking populations, fuelled by poor transport options. The tensions between levels of government, with their differing agendas and priorities, can create frustrations at the lowest level and can be the hardest issue to negotiate for entrepreneurial parish and town councils.

Nevertheless, small towns and rural areas remain some of the most active and dynamic hubs of the global municipalist movement, and are often the pioneers of election-winning municipalism in their respective countries. There are many examples of situations in which the bringing together of local businesses, schools, community groups and engaged citizens have brought about significant changes despite small budgets and limited powers.

Mini-manifesto

- **Don't be afraid to challenge the power of local political elites:** in small towns, often all it takes for seemingly entrenched political interests to be swept away is for a few committed people to create an alternative.

- **Propose concrete changes that affect local people's daily lives.** This helps to reduce stigma and lessen people's reservations about different ideological projects. The best way to engage people in the change we want to see in the world is to show them that it's possible at the local level and that we can make material changes to local residents' reality.
- **Make your municipalist platform as diverse as possible.** Encourage the involvement of a wide variety of people with diverse perspectives, skills and backgrounds.
- **Use social media as a listening and dialogue tool but don't forget to engage with people in person and through community and business groups and via public-sector bodies.** In a small town, in order to engage with the widest possible audience, use a variety of engagement methods – meetings, noticeboards and newspapers, as well as social media.
- **Be imaginative in the context of limited local powers.** In contexts of recentralization and austerity imposed by higher levels of government, it's vital to stretch the limits of what your local government *can* do and to be creative in thinking about how it can transform people's lives in small ways. Seek to bring together statutory services, community groups and commercial enterprises and build on the skills and interests of energetic residents to capitalize on local resources and 'do more with less'.
- **Facilitate residents' participation in decision-making** by providing them with as much information as possible and by making council and other meetings less pompous and more down to earth and action-oriented (for example, get rid of ceremonial procedures, hold meetings at times residents who work can attend, hold sessions in public spaces, and allow open debate).
- **Create a clear long-term vision and strategy to shape and select options and opportunities, and be bold.** Local councils can help to create an imaginative vision and can encourage the whole community to feel empowered and able to tackle 'big' issues – around prosperity, equality and sustainability.

- **Test out the limits of power.** Small councils may be able to borrow money, apply for grants and accept donations, and in so doing tackle bigger projects and initiatives than they would normally undertake.

Examples

SHARE, Independents for Frome (population 27,000), UK

SHARE is a 'library of things' set up by Frome Town Council in partnership with a local social enterprise, Edventure, and is an excellent example of the innovative, low-cost and participative projects that are common in Frome. The local council provided £7,000 ($9,000) of financing, and eight young people set up the initiative as part of specialist training in community entrepreneurship. SHARE is located in a previously empty shop let at a nominal rate to the council and is run primarily by volunteers.

The library recycles goods which would otherwise be thrown away and allows people to borrow items they do not use regularly or cannot afford, for a low fee. In its first month, over 300 items were donated or lent to the shop, and 60 members borrowed over 30 items, including a leaf blower, a record player, a projector, a PA system, toys and musical instruments. The space is also used for community events such as weaving and crocheting, and runs free training sessions on how to mend electrical goods. The manager also manages the community fridge, to which food from shops and restaurants can be donated and from which people in need can help themselves.

SHARE achieves multiple objectives – reducing waste, helping those with less income, creating social inclusion, maintaining traditional craft skills and providing training for young entrepreneurs. It costs very little to run and is a very good example of municipalism at work.

Collective governance, Autrement pour Saillans... tous ensemble (population 1,229), France

Since citizen municipalist platform Autrement pour Saillans took office in 2014, local government in Saillans has been entirely reformed to create a system of collegial and participatory governance between residents and town councillors. Power is shared: elected officials work in teams of two (or three) and make decisions within a steering committee open to the public. Residents can participate in defining policy priorities through issue-based commissions, and in implementing policies through Project Action Groups. Currently, 230 people, or 24 per cent of the population, participate in either a commission or a Project Action Group.

Municipal Office of People's Services, Candidatura d'Unitat Popular (CUP) de Celrà (population 5,300), Catalonia/Spain
The CUP municipal government made a significant investment to set up the Municipal Office of People's Services (Oficina Municipal d'Atenció a les Persones) so as to centralize all services for elderly people and their carers. The Office provides free psychological therapy and respite services for carers. It also has a member of staff dedicated to making 'good morning' check-up telephone calls to all the elderly people in the village every day, and to alerting their families if they don't respond. This initiative was made possible by the strong sense of community and social solidarity in the town.

Feminizing politics
Small towns and rural areas face particular challenges and have particular opportunities when it comes to feminizing politics, to promoting increased co-operation with, and participation and power-sharing by, people traditionally excluded from political life. On the one hand, socio-economic structures in rural areas often conform to traditional patterns, in which there are deep inequalities between the sexes in the division of care, domestic work, self-sufficient agriculture and paid work, making equal political participation even more difficult than in many cities. Furthermore, 'informal' and often tacit ways of holding power, which benefit males, can, paradoxically, be more prevalent in small towns and rural areas, where there are fewer formal roles and structures and a conservative or traditionalist culture.

On the other hand, small towns and rural areas can enjoy a greater sense of community and more of a culture of the commons than their urban counterparts. Mutual support between residents is both more necessary and more feasible in smaller, more isolated communities, and the need to manage common goods such as water and soil make the unit of the community more important than that of the individual or even local public administrations. Since women are central to community life, albeit often in deeply gendered roles, this can give them increased capacity to influence shared goals and ways of working. This area of the community governance of public and common goods provides an interesting opportunity to push the feminization of politics forward in small towns and rural areas, in terms of both participation and diversity in the political agenda.

Working as a global network

Kickstarting wider movements

New ways of working at local level, even in the smallest towns, can often spark interest on the national and indeed the international scene. Local experiments in new political processes will soon garner interest if they result in tangible changes to the community, as measured by prosperity (such as a reduction in empty premises or the establishment of street markets), increased focus on social and environmental issues (such as campaigns on becoming a plastic-free community), innovative local services (such as community transport schemes) and increased participation in public life. In this way, small communities such as Frome in the UK, Saillans in France or Torrelodones in Spain, can 'punch above their weight' and kickstart wider movements through showing what can be achieved. The national press is often seeking 'good news' stories and is keen to showcase such examples, and other communities wondering how to proceed are keen to visit these places and explore how they can make similar changes.

Tools and resources

Fearless Cities roundtable: 'Municipalism in Small Towns and Rural Areas'
youtu.be/M_taxF5XG00

Flatpack Democracy, A DIY guide to creating independent politics
Peter Macfadyen, 2014. A book on how to stand for local
office and challenge traditional political parties, based on the
experience of Independents for Frome.
flatpackdemocracy.co.uk

Municipalism: from citizen emancipation to shared political power
Institut de Recherche et Débat sur la Gouvernance, 2017
nin.tl/municipalisme

10

Creating non-state institutions

Rocio Novello (Ciudad Futura), **Sinam Mohammad** (Foreign Affairs Envoy of the Kurdistan Syrian Administration of northern Syria), **Kevin Buckland** (artivist for climate justice)

Work that comes from a position of mutualism, whether it be on self-organization, on town planning, on municipalism, or on the connections we may need to create a different society, can only be found under citizen governments, a form of organization that stops us from being state actors and that displays the limits of actual capitalism. This allows us to respond to several needs that are not currently being met and helps us build new forms of solidarity.
Mauro Pinto, Massa Critica, Naples, Italy

Is it important that non-state organizations are connected to political movements? For us, if they are not connected to a political project, then they cannot fulfil their transformative function… their experience will remain a part of the capitalist structure.
Sacajawea Hall, Cooperation Jackson, Jackson, US

Our years of experience of the relation between institutions and the street has shown us that the space available to transform society from within the institutions themselves is very small. We are therefore studying how to handle institutional representation and how these intermediate spaces are managed in order to bring about the social and political change that we seek.
Mariona Pascual, La Clau, Sant Celoni, Catalonia/Spain

Context

Events over the last 30 years have shown us that, at a global level, neoliberalism combines the dismantling of the state institutions that are alien to it, such as any that are concerned with redistribution, with the creation of new forms of institutional regulation and state management that are placed in the service of corporate interests. The neoliberalization process is built on sophisticated mechanisms with far-reaching political and cultural import, whose aim is to expropriate collective wealth and collective goods via the privatization of public property – whether the private owners are local or foreign. Neoliberal politics reduces the funding for public goods, and also reduces the amount of common wealth available, forcing us to look for different ways to protect the commons and challenging us to confront and overcome the urban corporate model, which builds cities that are unequal, fragmented, and determined by nothing more than the logic of the market.

We are convinced that this context obliges us to break with the hegemonic and binary mindset that can only conceive of a world run either by the state or by market forces. This notion, that the commons can only be managed by one of these two elements, is one we roundly reject: from our experience as activists we look for ways to imagine and build possible new ways of living. Our first great challenge is simply to enter into this way of thinking, to expand and interrogate the notion of public goods, given that these do not fully coincide with what is managed by the state. Public wealth comes in two forms: state-public (or managed by the state) and non-state-public (managed by non-state actors). If we think of things in this three-part way – state, market, non-state – then we can better consider the possibility that is in front of us (given that we are the majority) to achieve greater democratization and greater responsibility for the care and management of our common wealth.

Our aim is to conceive of social management as a political hypothesis for the city. We think that the idea of social management, with its capacity to deal with the multiple dimensions of communal urban life, will allow us the chance to model new ideas of the city, and of life in general. From popular assemblies to the creation of co-operatives, schools, cultural centres and financial instruments, our practice is developing and becoming more powerful, increasing the rights of citizens on our path towards true equality, and democratizing the space where decisions are taken as we move towards freedom.

Mini-manifesto

- **Build power that is different, that belongs to the people.** Our aim is to build a different kind of power, one that is more local but with untrammelled capacity to extend itself: our non-state institutions and our capacity for prefiguring our collective future are not just means to an end. They are both product and process, simultaneously. They come from our autonomy and exist in support of our autonomy. We are building the material support for a new form of government, which will feed on the empowerment provided to every person who lives in our cities. We talk of a power that is different: this is our guarantee, our way of protecting the advances that we are making, and keeping them as much as we can from regressive political contexts; it is this difference that makes it possible for us to win control of the cities, to take our model up to state level and inhabit the state from a point of view that is fairer and more equal.

- **Live today in the city of tomorrow.** Municipalism, self-government, mutual aid: these all allow us to create and inhabit, right here and right now, the society which we look for tomorrow, and prefigure our collective future. Beginning with concrete projects and winning little battles as they come up (creating schools, and education and cultural centres, for example) is a good way of showing in the present the power of the city of tomorrow.

- **Promote greater social innovation**. We know that it is not enough simply to oppose the injustices that permeate our society. We know that in order to attain the change we desire, we need to accompany every criticism with a concrete proposal, one that reveals the city we are dreaming of. We support non-state institutions because they allow us greater social innovation compared with traditional institutional politics.

- **Create a new relationship between institutions in order to protect and support the commons.** The state needs to respond and adapt to a new role in the face of the creation of non-state institutions. There is no consensus on how to deal with the state in all its forms. But we are in agreement on the need not only to reinvent the ways in which we participate in institutions but also to rethink the concepts and structures of the state, breaking down the walls that stop the public thinking in common.

- **Build a global network.** We do not want to create free and emancipatory microclimates which work for a limited number of individuals. Rather, we wish to build spaces that question their environment and build new ways of living. International and intra-municipal institutional spaces do exist, but people who are not inside them constantly come up against the lack of logistical resources to expand their collaborations and external networks. There is as yet no international space where non-state institutions can meet and develop their ideas. Such a space might very well be where non-state projects manage to become more than the sum of their parts, and a municipalist global network could manage and promote power at a scale that allowed it to defy the dominant paradigm of capitalist nation-states.

Examples

Rojava Municipalities and Environment Commission, Rojava Administration, northern Syria

After the revolution in Rojava and the withdrawal of government forces from the north of Syria, the municipal authorities in the Rojava region established in 2012 a series of commissions for basic services, with the aim of guaranteeing access to them. In a context of conflict, resistance and the struggle against terrorism, municipal authorities – via a democratic and co-operative administration – provided the services necessary for the community for a long period until the declaration of self-government in 2014 by an alliance of political forces representing the diversity of the population (Arabs, Kurds and Syrians). The Municipalities and Environment Commission was one of the most important commissions in this process of regional self-government, as it had the responsibility for organizing municipal areas in relation to political and environmental problems. This it did from a democratic standpoint, emphasizing the rights of women and a lack of tolerance for discrimination. Following elections, the commission continues to support municipal self-government.

Strategic projects for social management of common goods, Ciudad Futura, Rosario, Argentina

At the time of writing, Ciudad Futura is supporting several different examples of collective management, known as 'strategic projects'. These are non-state institutions and are made up of autonomous mechanisms within the wider political framework, involve local organizations, and work with the city's legislative bodies. Each one of these projects has its own organizational structure, its own way of taking decisions and its own way of managing its resources. They have revived the local milk industry, not just as a productive strategy, but also as a way of stopping evictions from the last pieces of undeveloped land in the city. They have also founded two schools for adults in areas of the city that had been abandoned by the state, while healthcare facilities have been set up in areas that have been devastated by urban violence and drug-trafficking. These institutions, along with the many others that exist in Rosario, are the nucleus of the future city which we hope to build tomorrow.

People's Assembly, Jackson, Mississippi, US

When the People's Assembly was set up in Jackson at the end of the 1980s, the city had high rates of poverty, was extremely socially deprived and was suffering cuts in public services. There was a clear need for a new and radical social force that could face up to this crisis. The Jackson People's Assembly was set up as a vehicle to empower residents of the city, in particular African-American residents, and to build self-governing social movements. The People's Assembly carried out projects that were independent of the government and necessary for the local population, and also petitioned the government to protect the interests of the population. This is a struggle that has continued up to the present day.

Nowadays, Cooperation Jackson is trying to build a network of co-operatives which will link together three interdependent organizations: an emerging federation of local workers' co-operatives; a group that helps co-operatives develop; and a centre for education and co-operative training (the Lumumba Center for Economic Democracy and Development). The organizers of Cooperation Jackson are certain that they can replace the current socio-economic system, based on exploitation, exclusion and the destruction of the environment, with a democratic alternative based on equality, co-operation, workers' democracy and environmental sustainability, and they try to reduce racial difference and generate communal wealth.

Feminizing politics

Within the framework of these processes of democratization, intensification and expansion of the capacity for social management of the commons (far beyond traditional state or market control of the same), the challenge to feminize politics is a serious one: there is no way of developing social autonomy without dismantling the sexist rationalizations behind previous models. This has to be done constructively, in a way that passes beyond simple denunciation and challenge, and which instead proposes concrete ways in which other ways of life can be organized that are fairer and more equal. The creation of non-state public institutions allows us to build on a foundation of leadership that is collective, organic and committed to a politics of the emotions, which puts the individual at the centre of the action, even allowing for the contradictions that we encounter every day.

Key concepts

Social management: Social management is the embodiment of new institutional methods; it is something that comes into being as soon as civil society organizes itself to act and move beyond the structures that the state seeks to impose. It represents a new horizon for citizen building that is autonomous, horizontal and collective. It provides the opportunity to create efficient ways for the commons to be managed by those who are closest to it. Social management contains within itself new forms of power and democracy.

Prefiguring: This is a term that should be understood as a way of acting so as to create future practices in the present. It is based on the idea that the process of creation of the project is a part of the project itself. We look for keys to building ways of life that are different from the hegemonic, and which set co-operation against competition, production against speculation, and a good life against the panic of hyperconsumption.

Tools and resources

Fearless Cities roundtable: 'Creating non-state institutions'
youtu.be/kcr-YZXHJ_U

POLICY
TOOLKITS

11

Radical democracy in the city council

Laura Roth (Barcelona En Comú), **Brad Lander** (Deputy Leader for Policy, New York City Council) and **Gala Pin** (Councillor for Participation and Districts, Barcelona City Council)

We don't believe in traditional formal representation. We're in the institutions with the goal of destroying them from within.
Áurea Carolina de Freitas, City Councillor, Belo Horizonte, Brazil

We cities are learning from one another; it's a liquid federation of direct democracy and participation.
Bernardo Gutiérrez, MediaLab Prado, Madrid, Spain

Context

It's easy to believe, at the moment, that people aren't interested in politics, or even that they don't value democracy. But that's not true. We want to have an active role in the decisions that affect our daily lives, our neighbourhoods and our communities. But we don't believe – and with good reason – that traditional electoral democracy is giving that to us. We don't think it's enough to just vote once every four years, and then let elected officials – too often captured by forces far from democratic accountability – make all the decisions for us.

We're searching for new forms of democratic decision-making, and that's where municipalism comes in. Municipalism is about more than implementing progressive local policies, it's about decentralizing power and giving communities the tools to make decisions collectively. The good news is that the local level offers opportunities for radical democracy that other levels of government do not: participation, transparency and accountability are easier to achieve on a smaller scale, and by institutions that are closer to the people. The issues dealt with at local level help too: we all want to be involved in making concrete decisions, however small, about the environments in which we actually live. Indeed, often small decisions – a new park in place of an empty plot of land, a new transportation connection that opens up vast new opportunities – can make a huge difference.

Greater local democracy can also improve democracy at the global level. Given that cities and local governments are becoming key actors in the political context we live in, making them more democratic has great potential to give ordinary people a voice in how to deal with global problems like speculation with housing, immigration, climate change and the reduction of poverty.

Nevertheless, the debate about the opportunities for and limits to different kinds of participation is far from over. One particular challenge is how to open up channels for the participation of ordinary people in decision-making, while at the same time making sure that the demands of social movements and associations are heard. City councils should aim to strengthen these movements and associations so they have the resources to make their demands known, and should ensure they have the effective means to influence decisions, monitor institutional action and contribute to policy design. At the same time they should empower ordinary citizens who do not want to or cannot become social activists.

Other unresolved questions include not only how to increase participation, but also how to make sure that we are taking care of the quality of decisions; how to combine digital and face-to-face democracy; how to engage people who aren't interested or don't have the time and resources; and how to convince public officials and representatives to give up power to ordinary people, among many other things.

Mini manifesto

- **Democracy means self-government. Delegation and representation are second best.** Treat communities as the real owners of the decision-making power, not just as sources of information or opinions.
- **Aim to make institutions less hierarchical, less bureaucratic and more transparent.** People cannot make decisions if the administration is too mysterious.
- **Acknowledge the potential exclusionary effect of any tool.** There is no one-size-fits-all solution. Establish different channels so that people with different capacities, interests and backgrounds can decide which ones they want to use.
- **Promote the use of digital infrastructures that can be re-appropriated** and make sure that they are accessible and people can learn how to use them. Combine them with face-to-face processes.
- **Motivate people to participate by actively offering them an opportunity that is real and effective.** Not everyone is an activist or a member of an association. Remember those who are not already mobilized, show them how their contribution can be effective, and let them know that you are not just seeking legitimacy but real effects and empowerment for them.
- **Build social connections and make participation fun.** Radical democracy is not just about outcomes. When it's done properly, people discover the joy of acting together in solidarity, across lines of difference. Making participation fun goes a long way.
- **Accept conflict** and don't aim at falsely resolving the deep struggles that constitute our complex societies.
- **Think in terms of participatory ecosystems** and not merely separate participatory tools. Find the way for tools to work together and reinforce one another.
- **Pay attention to the three kinds of effects of any decision-making procedure** and find ways to balance them if they conflict with each other:
  - Effect on the quality of the decision. Aim to make informed and reasoned decisions as far as possible.

- Effect on inclusion and equality. Aim to give everyone the same amount of power to influence decisions.
- Effect on the participants. People learn how to make decisions by making decisions themselves. Trust them and help them.
- **Promote radical democracy everywhere.** Create a democratic culture in local associations, political parties and companies.

Examples

Decidim Barcelona, Barcelona En Comú

This is a digital platform for participatory democracy that allows citizens to make proposals, deliberate on them, promote them and collectively defend and improve them. It was used to build the strategic plan for the city of Barcelona, and to develop some prototypes of processes such as participatory budgeting. In the future, it will also include the possibility of secure voting, for example in a referendum or as part of a consultation.

This is not only a great tool, but also a way of taking a stand against the use of technology as a business and the power of big corporations such as Google or Facebook. Decidim can be described as a 'zone of peace' that serves as a public forum in the middle of a global race to control information, public discourse and personal data. Decidim was designed in a collaborative way by civil society, academics and public officials. It is a radical free/open-source software/data/content project, so any institution or organization can use and further develop the software for free. The code can be found on GitHub and the (already internationalized) MetaDecidim community will help you and others install, develop and make the best use of it.

The platform supports processes with many thousands of participants. It also allows online and offline participation to be combined. Offline meetings can be announced online and the minutes can be added to the digital process. On Decidim participation is transparent, accessible and traceable. Neighbours can see what happens to their proposals, they can meet each other, organize themselves and fight for their rights.

Collective mandate, Belo Horizonte, Brazil

The collective mandate initiative was born from the lack of belief in traditional formal representation on the part of municipalist platform Muitas pela Cidade que Queremos. Instead of Muitas' city councillors just being chosen and then pushing for the implementation of their political manifesto, their actions are determined by a broader group, which consults ordinary citizens, social movements and activists on a regular basis. Eight members of the team were chosen through an open call in which 4,000 people stood as candidates, which was a way of opening up and democratizing the process even more.

The team is organized horizontally and offers advice to the two city councillors, working collectively to define their priorities and the positions they take in votes in the city council. The two representatives who are implementing the collective mandate participate in formal political institutions with the aim of transforming them from within. They're using institutional representation as a tool for experimenting with emancipatory political processes that allow collective decision-making.

Channels of dialogue were created to allow the mandate to be responsive to the city's key issues, including meetings in public spaces, laboratories for the creation of legislative proposals and an experimental theatre group. The main achievement of this experience is its inclusion of people who didn't have a say in public decision-making in the past, such as black people, women, the LGBT community, indigenous people and poor people. The collective mandate gives them an accessible channel for expressing their opinions and needs.

Participatory budgeting, from Porto Alegre to New York City

Participatory budgeting allows people to make direct decisions about how public money should be spent. People brainstorm ideas in neighbourhood assemblies. Grassroots budget delegates research projects and decide what goes on the ballot paper. Residents vote, and the winning projects are funded.

Participatory budgeting began in Porto Alegre more than two decades ago, and has spread to thousands of cities around the world. As with any democratic practice, it can become stale or get co-opted by particular interests. But with strong organizing, online and offline, it can empower disenfranchised people to transform their communities for the common good.

In New York City, voters in participatory budgeting ballots are much more likely than traditional voters to be low-income, people of colour, young, or non-citizens. They have created new parks, playgrounds and greenhouses in public-housing developments, sparked city-wide renovations of decrepit school washrooms, and engaged tens of thousands of diverse new activists.

Feminizing politics

Radical democracy is both an opportunity and a challenge. On the one hand, it allows for methods of decision-making that take some power from those who have the regulated professional knowledge or other kinds of recognized authority (usually men). It puts these decisions in the hands of those who will be directly affected by them in practice and who are usually excluded from political decision-making. In addition, some democratic processes, like deliberative ones, favour consensus-based decision-making, the exchange of ideas, learning about other people's situations and views, and accepting and dealing with diversity. But radical democracy also has a dark side. It's time-consuming, and this usually makes men more likely to participate than women. In addition, deliberation-based procedures need to take into account the fact that men's opinions are usually given greater weight and are better considered than women's, because of listeners' bias, as well as the fact that men are usually more confident in expressing their views and in speaking out in public, use more speaking time, and so on.

Working as a global network
Free open-source software
Decidim.Barcelona (Decidim) and Decide.Madrid (CONSUL)

were developed as free software and this allows other organizations and local governments to collaborate in developing online decision-making platforms, instead of competing with each other. Both platforms offer support and advice to organizations and institutions interested in using the software to create their own digital participation platforms. More than 50 local government bodies from all over the world are already using versions of Decidim or CONSUL (Helsinki, Turin, Buenos Aires, Porto Alegre, Pamplona and Gwangju, among others). For example, the Buenos Aires and the Paris Public Housing Company have used CONSUL to hold participatory budgeting processes.

The International Observatory on Participatory Democracy

This international network of local government bodies, academics and associations aims to promote participatory democracy at the local level. It works in co-operation with UCLG (United Cities and Local Governments) and helps municipalities to share, learn and evaluate decision-making procedures.

Key concepts

Deliberative democracy: decision-making procedures where the aim is to reach a consensus and the method is debate and discussion. People might change their point of view if they see there are better arguments than their own, or by taking the impact of the decision on other people into account.

Direct democracy: decision-making procedures where the final word is in the hands of those affected by the decision; for example, a consultation or a referendum.

Bottom-up approach to decision-making: an approach where decisions are made by those affected by them.

Tools and resources

Policy roundtable 'Radical Democracy in the City Council'
youtu.be/xm7xOTsKpK8

MetaDecidim The portal of the Decidim community.
Here you can learn about the tool, talk to other people using
it, propose new functionalities, and so on.
meta.decidim.barcelona

Portal about CONSUL, the software behind Decide. Madrid
consulproject.org/en

International Observatory on Participatory Democracy
oidp.net/en

12

Public space

Ana Méndez (Ahora Madrid), **Iva Marcetic** (Zagreb je NAŠ!),
Ksenija Radovanovic (Ne Da(vi)mo Beograd) and **Raquel
Rolnik** (architect and urbanist)

*It was totally spontaneous. We went to the riverbank to protect
something we hadn't even realized was ours.*
  Ksenija Radovanovic, Ne Da(vi)mo Beograd, Belgrade, Serbia

*The struggles in Belgrade or Berlin are the same. They're the
struggle between the idea of the territory as the common property
of city dwellers versus the idea of the territory as a playground for
international, financial capital. In this fight, all occupations, all
conflictual and self-made planning, all non-designed public spaces,
are meaningful outposts that are not only resisting and confronting,
but also prototyping, other ways of thinking about cities.*
  Raquel Rolnik, architect and urbanist

Context

Public space has been at the centre of some of the most iconic
urban struggles over recent years. From the new 'urban
frontier' of Tompkins Park Square in Manhattan, to Reclaim
The Streets in London, to the Arab Spring and the Occupy and
Indignados movements, the occupation of public space and the
resistance to its expropriation creates a collective idea of self-
organization, creativity and strength that defies the neoliberal
trope that 'there is no alternative'. It is no coincidence that
municipalist movements such as Pravo na Grad (Right to the
City) in Zagreb or Ne Da(vi)mo Beograd (Don't Let Belgrade
D(r)own) have been able to articulate the resistance against
the ubiquitous privatization and expropriation of public and

collective resources through struggles in defence of particular public spaces, whether they be squares or riverbanks.

Events such as the citizen-led occupation of Tempelhof Airport in Berlin and its transformation into a park in 2010 challenge the liberal and colonial notion of 'public' space as the private property of the government or the state. They are founded on the idea of public space as a common space: open, accessible, democratic, and meeting our individual and collective needs. For it to really belong to everybody, public space should allow self-managed, confrontational processes that defy the traditional construction of 'clean' and non-conflictual space and produce common spaces where collective rules are defined and continually transformed by their users and inhabitants. Contesting the traditional idea of public space requires us to experiment with new ways of thinking about, designing and inhabiting it.

Public spaces create collective symbols, provide the opportunity for social encounters, and act as a political forum. They can host marketplaces and open-air showrooms, games and conversations, protests and rallies, music and fairs. When designed with care, they can also provide security and protection. Streets and squares are not just physical infrastructure; they are cultural, economic and political resources. As such, they can be vehicles for exclusion, inequality and disenfranchisement or for solidarity, empowerment and democracy.

As a resource that is directly regulated by local governments, public space (and the question of who gets to decide what happens in it, and how) is a central concern of the municipalist movement. Because public space is regulated, not just by local rules and by-laws, but also by social norms that are the result of continual public negotiation, local governments can play a key role as arbiters of everyday activities and promoters of inclusive spaces, as well as by enabling and encouraging communal governance.

Mini-manifesto

- **Design public space for and with the people**, through participatory, open-ended and co-designed processes that involve citizens, professionals and public workers.

- **Make public space accessible** for all kinds of diverse bodies and needs, with ramps where necessary, public water fountains, public toilets, and so on.
- **Use tangible, concrete issues** relating to public space to understand, explain and challenge systemic economic and political problems in your community.
- **Make public spaces feel safe** (especially for women) by designing them to be busy, welcoming and connected rather than empty, inhospitable and isolated.
- **Prevent the commodification of public space** by controlling its commercial use, preventing mono-functional uses and limiting advertising.
- **Promote the production of public space as commons.**
- **Be aware of the relationship of public space to the right to housing**, and design public spaces in a way that helps to prevent, rather than provoke, the gentrification of surrounding areas.

Examples

Movements to protect public space, Zagreb and Belgrade

In recent years, both Zagreb and Belgrade have given birth to mass urban movements opposed to the privatization of public space. In 2014, Ne Da(vi)mo Beograd (Don't Let Belgrade D(r)own) was set up to oppose the corruption-ridden, speculative Waterfront project on the banks of the River Sava. At its peak, the movement organized protests of up to 20,000 people, and succeeded in raising awareness about both the Waterfront project and urban development policy in the city more broadly.

The campaign 'We Won't Give Away Varsavska Street' in Zagreb sprang up in 2006 in reaction to the redevelopment of the central Flower Market Square to meet the needs of private investors. The campaign lasted four years and encompassed 80 actions, including protests, occupations and civil disobedience, which mobilized up to 10,000 people at a time.

While neither campaign achieved its immediate aim of stopping redevelopment, both served as processes of collective empowerment and education and as the basis for the creation of municipalist election candidacies in both cities. The experiences of Zagreb and Belgrade show that when public space is understood as the common property of citizens, rather than as the private property of the government, movements to defend it have the potential to generate wide social support and to trigger the desire for a more open and democratic city.

Almendro 3, Madrid

We've grown up in empty lots
in places taken over by the neighbourhood
We conquered small territories
planting mountains, treasures, words in each of them
and all of us: mothers, fathers, neighbours, friends, schools, lovers
We all play at rethinking how to make the city.

Manifesto hung at the gate of Almendro 3

Almendro 3 is a formerly abandoned plot of land, redeveloped by and for children in the centre of Madrid. The site had long been used by residents of the La Latina neighbourhood as a refuge from the hectic tourist activity in the city centre, when, in 2015, the city council proposed turning it into a cultural space. A counter-proposal presented by local residents and children highlighted the value of empty plots as playgrounds and suggested developing the space through collaborative thinking and design.

The council responded by launching a participatory process, guided by Zuloark, a group of architects and designers. Weekly meetings were held where children helped to design the space and parents discussed questions of governance and responsibility. Madrid City Council facilitated the process, making minimal architectural changes and allowing the different activities, discussions and issues to follow their natural course.

The main use of Almendro 3 is now as a recreation area for children and elderly people. It has a fountain and sandpit, as well as benches on the slopes that also accommodate plants brought in from the municipal nursery, among which there are palm trees, hedges, seasonal flowers, boxwoods and aromatic plants.

Feminizing politics

Against a backdrop of towns and cities that have been designed for a 'neutral' human being, as defined by the male-dominated urban planning profession, feminist urbanism recognizes women as a source of unique knowledge about the city. This approach seeks to provide spaces and tools for women to reflect on how the built environment is transformed, how it transforms them through their everyday lives, and how they can take part in the production of the city: from the introduction of gender criteria to urban planning, to the promotion of women's participation in the design of public space.

One such initiative is the Women Safety Audits, developed at the end of the 1980s by the Metropolitan Action Committee on Violence Against Women and Children in Toronto. The audits, which were conducted through exploratory walks around the city to identify places where women felt unsafe or had experienced harassment or aggression, were based on the assumption that women are experts on their own safety and that collaboration between women's movements and local government was necessary to drive change. This idea was taken up in Spain by the feminist collective Plazandreok, which published its own 'Map of the Forbidden City' in 1996 to analyse women's experience of public space in San Sebastián/Donostia.

More recently, the global Hollaback! movement has allowed women and LGBTQ individuals to report and map any street harassment they experience or witness in real time using a mobile app. Set up in New York in 2005, Hollaback! aims to change the culture regarding street harassment by enabling people to publicly report their harassers and express their outrage and their solidarity with one another. There are currently Hollaback! groups operating in 79 cities in 26 countries.

Working as a global network
Jane's Walks
Named after the urbanist Jane Jacobs (1916-2006) and held in the first weekend of May, around the time of her birthday, Jane's Walks are self-organized citizen-led walking conversations that aim to share not only architectonic characteristics of public space, but also questions related to culture, memory and history and social struggles. They encourage people to share stories about their neighbourhoods, discover unseen aspects of their communities, and use walking as a way to connect with their neighbours.

Since its inception in 2007, thousands of people have taken part in this worldwide public-space festival. In 2017 walks were held in over 200 cities in 41 countries.

Tools and resources
Fearless Cities roundtable: 'Public Space'
youtu.be/QZA0Mmn_xtM

Hollaback! Digital platform that allows people to report sexual harassment in public spaces.
ihollaback.org

Jane's walks
janeswalk.org

European Letter of the Women in the City
nin.tl/habitat

13

Housing, gentrification and tourism

Paula Marqués (Councillor for Housing and Urban Development, Lisbon), **Chloe Eudaly** (Commissioner, Portland City Council, Oregon) and **Vanessa Valiño** (Adviser in the Housing Department, Barcelona City Council)

What does it mean to be a city? A city is not first and foremost a tourist attraction or an investment vehicle for the global super-rich. If anything, a city should be about housing people. Without permanent rent regulation we're in danger of becoming nothing more than a Swiss Bank for the super-rich, and nothing more than a marketplace of short-term rentals.

Ritchie Torres, Deputy Leader, New York City Council

Legal instruments are not a protection in themselves. They're just a tool, and they're only as good as the people in City Hall. You need them to be used, and that's more likely when there are broad, strong social movements.

Andrej Holm, Professor of Urban Sociology at Humboldt University, Berlin

Context

Our towns and cities have become sites of global speculation. Housing is a basic necessity and the foundation of our communities, but international investors are treating it as a commodity, as something to be bought and sold for profit. As a result, ordinary people are facing unsafe conditions, rising rents, shorter contracts, evictions and homelessness. In many cities, short-term rental platforms like Airbnb are putting additional pressure on the supply of residential accommodation, pushing rents skyward and emptying neighbourhoods of local life. Housing insecurity is no longer a problem that affects just those on the lowest incomes.

Too often, victims of the global housing crisis are made to feel that their situation is the result of an individual failing, that it's something they should feel ashamed of. A municipalist approach can help us to politicize the seemingly private, domestic sphere of housing and reveal the collective nature of the problem. When we make this conceptual leap from the individual to the community, our neighbourhoods become the front line of the battle between ordinary people and global capital, the place where we can start to fight back, together, for the right to housing and the right to the city.

We want to guarantee the right to housing and defend our neighbourhoods. This means stopping evictions and cracking down on the harassment and intimidation tactics used by landlords and developers. We want housing to be genuinely affordable, so that people don't have to choose between paying their rent and buying other basic necessities, and so that they aren't forced to move out of their neighbourhoods. We want to fight phenomena like gentrification and 'touristification', which displace communities, segregate our cities and destroy the diversity and vitality of our neighbourhoods.

Mini-manifesto

- **End the criminalization of homelessness** and understand homelessness as part of a broad spectrum of housing insecurity, rather than as an isolated phenomenon.
- **Fight forced evictions** by informing tenants and mortgage-holders about their rights, providing institutional support in conflicts with landlords and banks, and through direct action.
- **Use rent control and urban planning** to limit speculative property investment.
- **Expand the stock of public housing** by purchasing buildings and land, constructing new units and repurposing existing municipal land and property.

- **Destigmatize public housing** by making it available to people from a range of socioeconomic backgrounds.
- **Regulate the land and rental markets** to discourage speculation and promote affordable housing.
- **Use fines and incentives** to discourage property owners from keeping their housing empty, and encourage landlords to provide longer-term, more affordable rental contracts.
- **Improve local data** on housing, to improve knowledge about the situation in each municipality.
- **Regulate short-term rentals** and sanction property owners and online platforms that break the rules.
- **Make sure that conservation policies in historic neighbourhoods protect the residential function of these areas** from speculation based on their value as tourist destinations.
- **Implement urban rehabilitation policies,** in order to encourage landowners to reclassify their assets, retain tenants and charge affordable rents.
- **Expand home-ownership opportunities** for low-income tenants, to stabilize families in the long term and to expand the capacity of rental stock.

Examples

The Assembly of Neighbourhoods for Sustainable Tourism and the Special Tourist Accommodation Plan, Barcelona

In 2017, Barcelona approved its Special Urban Plan for Tourist Accommodation (known as the PEUAT), a zoning plan designed to prevent further touristification of the city by regulating hotel and tourist apartment licences. The PEUAT is an example of how strong social movements can help a city government to adopt more ambitious measures on housing.

In the years preceding the PEUAT, movements critical of touristification (such as La Barceloneta Diu Prou, Fem Sant Antoni and Al Poblenou Ens Plantem) started to spring up in neighbourhoods across Barcelona. These movements started working to highlight the role of tourism in rent increases and to combat hotel developments. In 2015, these local platforms came together in the Assembly of Neighbourhoods for Sustainable Tourism (Assemblea de Barris per un Turisme Sostenible, ABTS) to advocate for the right to housing at city level.

The Barcelona government's initial PEUAT proposal established a 'degrowth' zone in the historic city centre, an ambitious goal, given the reluctance of most political parties in the City Council to limit the growth of the hotel sector. However, when the plan went out for consultation, the ABTS was able to mobilize its supporters and put pressure on all parties in the City Council to vote to extend the degrowth zone to include more neighbourhoods, making the final PEUAT even more effective than originally planned.

Portland Tenants United and The Shed, Portland, Oregon

In 2016, housing rose to the top of the political agenda in Portland. Rents had climbed 30 per cent over the previous four years. According to the city's annual *State of Housing* report, a median-priced two-bedroom apartment in Portland was beyond the reach of the average household in nearly half the city's neighbourhoods, and the average Latino, Black, Native American and single-parent households couldn't afford the median rent in any neighbourhood.

The crisis gave rise to a wave of citizen action, including the creation of Portland Tenants United (PTU), an ad-hoc tenants' group that picketed landlords while pushing for rent control and an end to no-cause evictions. Around the same time, a Facebook group, 'That's a Goddamned Shed', inspired by an advertisement asking $950 a month for a shed, quickly drew 2,000+ members and became a hub for information and resources and a springboard for local activism. PTU, in collaboration with other housing advocacy groups, staged rallies to help tenants in crisis, and policed local Craigslist rental adverts, many of which were illegal, had identifiable code violations, or violated the Fair Housing Act. They also launched a public campaign to 'Keep Portland Housed', which called for the passage of a Tenants' Bill of Rights and a moratorium on no-cause evictions and rent increases.

In November 2016, these grassroots mobilizations started to

have electoral consequences: Portland voters overwhelmingly approved a $258-million bond for affordable housing and elected renter and 'Shed' founder, Chloe Eudaly, as a City Commissioner on a housing rights platform.

Since then, there have been significant changes to housing policy in Portland, including the game-changing ordinance on Mandatory Renter Relocation Assistance, which obliges landlords to pay relocation assistance of between $2,900 and $4,500 to tenants who are served a no-cause eviction or a rent increase of 10 per cent or higher in a 12-month period. This new law has provided stability for thousands of tenants, including those whose entire apartment complexes were receiving rent increases of over 100 per cent or no-cause evictions, when the landlords were attempting to replace low-income families with higher-income renters moving to Portland.

The city has also created an Office of Rental Services and plans to create programmes to mediate in disputes between tenants and landlords, and to require all landlords in the city to register. A Rental Services Commission serves as the primary public forum for discussion of rental housing law and regulation, and for renter-owner programmes and services.

Guaranteed legal services for tenants facing eviction, New York City

In August 2017, New York City became the first US city to guarantee lawyers to tenants served with an eviction notice, with the goal of allowing tenants the same opportunity as landlords to defend their interests. Under the law passed by the City Council, legal services are provided to tenants facing eviction who make below 200 per cent of the federal poverty line ($50,000 per year), meaning more than 80 per cent of eviction cases qualify for legal assistance. The programme is being phased in over a five-year period and once fully implemented will have an annual budget of $155 million.

The policy followed a decades-long campaign for improved legal support by the tenant legal services community, which came together to create the Right to Council NYC Coalition in 2014. The Coalition successfully campaigned for greater funding for legal representation for tenants, managing to increase the percentage of tenants who appear before housing court with representation from just 1 per cent in 2013 to around 27 per cent in 2016. The Coalition hailed the move to guarantee legal services as a ground-breaking victory in the fight against wrongful evictions and called on other US cities to follow in New York's footsteps.

Feminizing politics

A feminist approach to housing takes into account the fact that women's lives are characterized by multiple inequalities, such as the feminization of poverty, sexist violence (which can create emergencies that force them to leave their homes), and care work (for example, most single parents are women). This results in significant differences in how they experience life in the city and means that housing policy must be based on the creation of communities that can provide the networks of care and support on which life depends.

Women have played a leading role in the struggle for the right to housing in many towns and cities; while their male partners have sunk into despair, many women have taken the lead in defending their homes, negotiating with banks, and taking direct action to stop evictions. These processes have been personally and collectively empowering for many women and have served to create new models of social and political leadership.

Working as a global network

European Action Coalition for the Right to Housing and to the City

The European Action Coalition for the Right to Housing and to the City is a network of movements from different cities across Europe that fight for these fundamental rights. After having campaigned locally for years, those movements (of tenants, slum or self-built neighbourhood dwellers, squat residents, victims of inadequate housing, eviction or indebtedness, and professionals and researchers) came together to take common action and agree common positions on housing issues at the European level. The coalition has undertaken joint, decentralized actions to denounce ventures such as the MIPIM real estate fair and the Blackstone vulture fund.

Key concepts

Gentrification: a process through which the arrival of new residents from a higher socioeconomic background to a neighbourhood causes rents and property prices to rise, often displacing lower-income residents and communities.

Touristification: a process through which the short-term rental of housing to tourists, particularly via online platforms, leads to an increasing proportion of properties in a neighbourhood being used as holiday, rather than residential, accommodation. Rather than replacing one type of resident with another, as in the case of gentrification, touristification replaces residents with a transient population of visitors. This can have a significant impact on commerce and services aimed at local residents.

Tools and resources

Special Tourist Accommodation Plan, Barcelona
nin.tl/tourism

The PAH Green Book: A basic guide to the PAH platform for people affected by mortgages
nin.tl/PAH

'Flat detector': Barcelona City Council site to help you spot whether you are staying in an illegal holiday rental
nin.tl/flatdetector

14

The commons

Laia Forné (Participation Advisor, Barcelona City Council), **Giuseppe Micciarelli** (Massa Critica, Naples) and **Iolanda Fresnillo** (La Hidra Cooperativa, Barcelona)

When we talk about commons, we're talking about communities that are organized around shared resources according to democratic forms of governance.

Iolanda Fresnillo, Ekona, Barcelona

Today management is often much more powerful than property, and management is the place where the commons are exploited and destroyed, so if we want to defend the commons we must imagine an alternative form of governance.

Giuseppe Micciarelli, Massa Critica, Naples

Context

Too often, the governance of our towns and cities has been based on an alliance between local governments and markets that prioritizes the exchange value of urban resources and pays little attention to their use value to residents. This has led to the increasing commodification of our cities, and a lack of democratic control mechanisms and measures to protect basic resources like public space, cultural centres, housing, food, transport and leisure services from the market.

Yet, around the world, communities have been resisting commodification processes by actively creating alternative governance models. Through these community practices, or 'commons', people are finding ways to manage collective resources on a democratic, not-for-profit basis. Since the commons are understood as the collective action used to govern resources, they can be found in innumerable areas of life. While the original conception of the commons was rural, referring to the communal management of forests, mountains and pastures, today one of the most prolific types of commons is found in the digital realm, in open-source software and crowd-sourced digital resources, such as Wikipedia.

Municipalism provides us with an opportunity to play with different ways of being a public institution; with forms of governance that make a clear commitment to the public-community management of the urban commons. Some cities, such as Naples, Kobane, Cochabamba and Barcelona, have a strong heritage of community management and self-managed projects. But even in towns and cities where the commons is still a relatively new idea, there's a growing demand by citizens for the recognition of the urban commons and for a greater ability to participate in the management and use of public resources and heritage.

Local institutions have often seen demands for community control of resources as problems or conflicts to manage. But the commons have sparked a debate about the relationship between the public-state, private-commercial and public-community spheres. We need a shift in thinking, so that the commons are seen as an opportunity to experiment with new forms of interaction between municipal governments and community initiatives. The commons shouldn't be understood as a substitute for public management, but as part of a democratizing process that emerges from strong community organization in a particular place.

The challenge is to maintain communal values (autonomy, usage rights, democratic management) while, at the same time, guaranteeing the principles of public services (accessibility, universality, transparency, public accountability). Redistribution isn't just about sharing resources, it's about giving people the power to directly manage public goods.

Mini-manifesto

- **Recognize and protect the commons that already exist** in our towns and cities as emerging commons, respecting the self-managed nature of these projects and conserving their social and economic value.

- **Create an institutional framework** that recognizes and incentivizes the collective and community construction and direct management of public goods, guaranteeing the public and participatory use of these resources in the pursuit of the common good.
- **Develop redistribution and social-justice mechanisms** that ensure equitable access to public goods and the recognition of knowledge as a common good, favouring collective and open-access modalities of knowledge property.
- **Create community monitoring mechanisms** that allow participants to (self-)evaluate their projects and gain awareness of areas in which they could improve their work for the community.
- **Foster a new relationship** between public administrations and citizens that pursues the 'direct administration' of projects by the people, governed by the principles of universality, accessibility, sustainability, transparency, and a democratic governance.

Examples

L'Asilo: from squatting to a new legal status, Naples

In 2015, Naples City Council adopted a series of measures to regulate, promote and institutionalize the urban commons. The measures aimed to allow the legal recognition of self-managed spaces and to enable the citizen management of buildings that belonged to the city council. The process emerged from an experiment involving the collective use of L'Asilo, an abandoned historic building owned by the municipality and declared a World Heritage Site by UNESCO.

On 2 March 2012, a group of cultural workers and citizens occupied L'Asilo, initially with the goal of holding cultural activities over a period of three days. Eventually, they decided to justify the self-management of L'Asilo 'for the civic use of a public good', in accordance with an Italian law that, while in disuse, was still in force. That was the first step in what was to become an unprecedented legal innovation. By means of a municipal ordinance, Naples City Council incorporated the concept of the 'emerging commons' into its statutes, and put rules for the use of certain types of properties, which were written by participants in the assembly occupying L'Asilo, into its regulatory framework.

The ability of L'Asilo activists to use the law to turn existing public/private management structures on their head in their city was an important milestone. In the period between May 2012 and June 2016, five more decisions made by Naples City Council, based on the legal work of the activists, recognized this governance model, which now applies to buildings covering an area of almost 40,000 square metres across the city. Other cities, such as Turin and Palermo, as well as social movements (including Mondeggi Fattoria Senza Padroni and Casa Bettola Reggio Emilia) have adopted this new legal tool, which allows citizens to use municipal infrastructure, guarantees access to it, and sets basic rules for its use.

Community use and management of citizen assets, Barcelona

Barcelona City Council's urban commons development policy includes the transfer of municipal assets to communities for the creation of social and cultural projects, the community management of public buildings and services, and the remunicipalization of basic services through mechanisms that allow for citizen participation and accountability.

Within this framework, the city has created the Community Use and Management of Citizen Assets Programme (Programa Patrimoni Ciutadà d'Ús i Gestió Comunitària). In collaboration with community spaces in the city of Barcelona, the programme has set criteria to define the framework that regulates access to, and transfer of, municipal assets and created a new self-evaluation mechanism, the 'Community Monitor' (Balanç Comunitari). The programme also includes the development of an audit of public assets (land and buildings) in order to create a catalogue of properties that are managed by the community.

The initiative was made possible by the establishment of

the Citizen Asset Board, a joint municipal body whose role is to co-ordinate the most important municipal departments related to the cession of municipal assets to non-profit organizations.

596 Acres, New York City

596 Acres was set up in 2011 when its founder, Paula Segal, came upon a city planning department spreadsheet which revealed that there were 596 acres of vacant public land in the borough of Brooklyn, much of it in some of the lowest-income neighbourhoods. She decided to use the data to create a map to display on posters around the city and put online. According to Segal, 'We started as an experiment in getting information about land ownership into the hands of people who really were ready to make change.'

Once the information was out there, New Yorkers wanted to find out how to access land and mobilize to protect parcels that were under threat. In response, 596 Acres developed a community land access advocacy programme to support neighbourhood campaigns to transform vacant plots throughout New York City into gardens, farms and play spaces.

The organization went on to turn its original online map into an interactive organizing tool, Living Lots NYC, which shows where people have access to land and where people are organizing to liberate land for community use and management. 596 Acres has since expanded its activity beyond vacant plots to include inaccessible and neglected parks, buildings and post offices.

Feminizing politics

The commons help communities to value the work of social reproduction, as they are based on promoting use values over market values. They are an exercise in democracy in that their management is based on equal, accessible and horizontal organizational structures.

We must be aware, though, of the risks of reproducing the gender stereotypes and inequalities in social reproduction in the structures of commons initiatives, something that is not assured by creating horizontal and accessible organizations alone, but which requires a specific gender approach.

Working as a global network

European Commons Assembly

In November 2016, a group of 150 people from all over Europe gathered in Brussels to create the European Commons Assembly, with the goal of laying the foundations for trans-local solidarity within the European commons movement. The European Commons Assembly has three main goals:

1 Support the decentralized activities of commoners and their engagement in concrete, collaborative and bottom-up actions.
2 Give a voice to and increase the visibility of the commons movement.
3 Channel the needs and demands of socially and ecologically sustainable initiatives to the political arena.

Tools and resources

Fearless Cities policy roundtable: 'Commons'
youtu.be/pO6y9Ytmj_Q

Remix the commons An intercultural space for sharing and co-creating multimedia documents about the commons.
remixthecommons.org/?lang=en

Rules for the civic use of L'Asilo, Naples
nin.tl/Asilo

15

Mobility and pollution

Andrea Reimer (Councillor for Environmental Action, Vancouver City Council), **César Ochoa** (Barcelona En Comú), **Francesco Luca Basile** (Civic Coalition for Bologna) and **Amaranta Herrero** (Barcelona En Comú)

'Some' is not a number and 'soon' is not a time; we need measurable indicators and mandatory reporting to reduce carbon emissions and pollution in our cities.

Andrea Reimer, Councillor for Environmental Action,
Vancouver City Council

We need to put this problem on our local agenda, but also on the agenda of the municipalities that surround us, as well as on regional and national government agendas. Air doesn't recognize administrative borders, so we need everyone on board for the fight against air pollution.

Janet Sanz, Fifth Deputy Mayor for Ecology,
Urban Planning and Mobility, Barcelona

Context

Mobility is a foundation of the right to the city, particularly for those living on the outskirts of large metropolitan areas, or in isolated towns and villages. Restricted mobility means restricted access to employment, education, leisure and services. The problem is that, too often, our cities and regions have been designed for cars instead of for people. Public investment has been ploughed into the construction of highways, tunnels and car parks rather than public transport and cycling and walking infrastructure. At a local level, this car-centred approach has given us air and noise pollution, injuries and deaths caused by road accidents, and public spaces invaded by private vehicles. It has also led to social and economic segregation, with those privileged enough to live in urban centres or to have access to private vehicles enjoying increased opportunities compared to everyone else. At a global level, this carbon-intensive model of urban development has contributed to putting us on the brink of a climate apocalypse, threatening the very existence of life on Earth.

We understand mobility not just as a technical issue, but also as a question of health and environmental and social justice. Over 90 per cent of the global population lives in areas where air-quality guidelines are not met. Air pollution is responsible for an estimated 6.5 million deaths a year worldwide, according to the World Health Organization. Air pollution is also correlated with cognitive problems in children and early-onset Alzheimer's. Transport emissions are the second-largest source of carbon-dioxide emissions and a leading cause of climate change. People who travel by car are more likely to be male and white, and to have higher-than-average incomes, meaning that car-based models of urban and territorial development reinforce gender, ethnic and economic inequalities. That's why we take an ecofeminist approach to mobility, putting people and the planet at the centre of how we design and connect our neighbourhoods, towns and cities.

Municipalism allows us to challenge unsustainable, high-carbon models of urban development, provide healthy, sustainable alternatives, and reverse the unfair system that gives the greatest freedom and mobility to the biggest polluters and those with the most resources.

We have to challenge the idea that driving is a right, stand up to the car lobby, and work to shift public attitudes and our transport culture. We want compact, walkable and cyclable cities, with public transport that is powered by renewable energy and accessible to all.

Mini-manifesto

- **Stand up to the car lobby** for the collective right to clean air.
- **Change the priorities of urban design** to put pedestrians

first and discourage private vehicle use.

- **Reduce the amount of public space dedicated to private vehicles** through measures like pedestrianization and repurposing parking spaces for alternative uses.
- **Promote public transport** through public investment and affordable fares that encourage frequent use.
- **Increase cycling** by creating, extending or improving bike lanes and by providing public bike-sharing systems.
- **Penalize or ban the use of high-emission vehicles** by creating low-emission zones where the most polluting vehicles are forbidden from entering (on a temporary or permanent basis).
- **Introduce congestion charges** for private vehicles entering city centres and increase the price of parking to reduce car use and fund investment in sustainable transport infrastructure.
- **Invest in a low-emission public transport fleet** in order to reduce energy consumption and CO_2 emissions per capita.
- **Create exclusive bus lanes** to increase the average speed of buses.
- **Encourage car-sharing** to reduce the number of vehicles on the road.
- **Set lower speed limits** to reduce pollution and accidents, e.g. 30 km/h in built-up areas

Examples

Greenest City Action Plan, Vancouver

In 2008, local platform Vision Vancouver was elected on a pledge of making Vancouver the greenest city in the world by 2020. In 2009, the local government announced that it was drawing up a Greenest City Action Plan, to prepare Vancouver for the potential impacts of climate change while building a vibrant community, a thriving green economy, and a greener, healthier city. The plan's participatory development and implementation have been essential to its high impact. Over 35,000 local residents (around 5 per cent of the city's population) participated in its design through regular meetings over a period of two years, and over 180 civil-society organizations, unions and academic institutions were involved. The plan includes hundreds of actions led by residents, as well as by the local government.

The plan includes 10 ambitious goals with 17 indicators and mandatory annual reporting. Its targets include reducing CO_2 emissions from 2007 levels by a third by 2020 and for all buildings constructed from 2020 onwards to be carbon-neutral in their operation. By April 2015, the city had already hit the target of over 50 per cent of journeys being made on foot, by bicycle or on public transport.

Thanks to the plan, Vancouver went from not featuring in the top 500 greenest cities in the world, to ranking fourth according to the global green index. This was achieved over the course of a decade in which the Conservative government in Canada pursued carbon-based development and withdrew the country from the international Kyoto Protocol on climate change. The national average of annual CO_2 emissions per capita in Canada is 15 tons; in Vancouver it's been reduced by 22 per cent to its current level of 3.9 tons. That's the difference a city can make.

AriaPesa grassroots air pollution measurement, Bologna

In 2017, the air in Bologna exceeded recommended limits of particulate matter, ozone and nitrogen dioxide, the last mainly as a result of vehicle emissions. The municipalist platform Coalizione Civica per Bologna (Civic Coalition for Bologna), which won two seats on the city council and four in the municipalities in the 2016 elections, has a strategy of 'leading from the opposition' on this and other issues. Coalizione Civica supports the AriaPesa (HeavyAir) citizen network, which aims to empower people through grassroots science. AriaPesa provides air-sampling sensors for residents to install near their homes to measure and map air pollution. Over 350 sensors have been installed around the city by individuals, schools, neighbourhood associations and the university, as well as by the official institute for air quality monitoring. The residents of Bologna are using the crowd-sourced data to support their calls to change city policy, improve air quality and protect human health.

Superblocks, Barcelona

In Barcelona, under 25 per cent of all trips in the city are made by car but around 70 per cent of public space is dedicated to driving and parking. Superblocks are an attempt to redress this imbalance by restricting the access of private vehicles to certain blocks of streets and creating new public 'squares' at the junctions of these pedestrianized roads. Only residential traffic, services, emergency vehicles and delivery vehicles (under special circumstances) are allowed to enter Superblocks, and even then they must stick to a 10 km/hr speed limit. Superblocks are oases in the densely populated urban landscape, providing space for community life, green space, sport and exercise.

When the most recent Superblock was set up in the neighbourhood of Poblenou, in 2016, local residents who supported the initiative came together to form the Col·lectiu Superilla (Superblock Collective). The group participates in the City Council's evaluation of the project and makes suggestions about how to use the reclaimed public space. One of the ideas that has been adopted was to install playgrounds in two of the four squares created at the junctions within the Superblock.

Feminizing politics

The impact of urban planning and transport policy is not gender-neutral. Our towns and cities have been designed around participation in the labour market, with little or no consideration of care and reproductive work. This bias is clearly evident in transport systems around the world, which tend to be set up for the convenience of twice-a-day commuters travelling long distances (a majority of whom are men), rather than for the benefit of caregivers and part-time workers (who are more likely to be women), who, typically, make multiple, short journeys. Transport infrastructure is often inaccessible to those who have mobility restrictions or travel with dependants, and women are at particular risk of sexual harassment and assault in public spaces when travelling on foot, by bicycle or on public transport. Feminizing mobility policy means challenging the privileges of private car users, giving equal importance to the transport needs of those engaged in reproductive work, and making travel on foot and public transport over short distances convenient, accessible, affordable and safe.

Working as a global network

ICLEI Ecomobility Alliance

The global network of local governments for sustainability, ICLEI, co-ordinates the Ecomobility Alliance, a network of towns and cities that promotes sustainable mobility. The Alliance has created a set of 20 indicators of sustainable mobility called Ecomobility SHIFT, which member towns and cities can use to measure the ecological impact of their transport infrastructure and identify ways to improve it.

Tools and resources

Fearless Cities roundtable: 'Mobility and pollution'
youtu.be/6DqCI7Azwnk

'"Superblocks": Let's Fill the Streets with Life'
Barcelona City Council webpage
nin.tl/superblocks

Ecomobility SHIFT system of indicators to measure and improve sustainable mobility in cities
ecomobility.org/ecomobility-shift

16

Remunicipalization of basic services

Moises Subirana (Barcelona En Comú), **Claire Roumet** (Director, Energy Cities) and **Olivier Petitjean** (Observatoire des multinationales)

Remunicipalization has been forced into being by a concern for ecological sustainability, democracy and social justice, and as a response from municipalities to the politics of austerity.
Olivier Petitjean, Observatoire des multinationales

The battle for public water supplies has begun, a battle between citizens and extremely strong corporate interests.
Miriam Planas, Aigua és Vida, Catalonia

In the process of remunicipalization private lobbies are strong players.
Miguel Penas, Co-ordinator of the Mayor's Office, Santiago de Compostela

Context

After three decades of mass privatization of public services, the situation is not good. The neoliberal recipe for the public sector, which it considered bureaucratic, centralized, inefficient and obsolete, has ended up being accused of the same defects. Worse still, privatization has given transnational corporations more power than the public institutions they claim to be serving.

In the face of this situation, more and more cities and towns have decided to institute structural changes in the way they provide education, health services, water and electricity.

117

In spite of the many legal obstacles which are frequently imposed on them by the state, municipalities are opting for methods of management that, based on a broad understanding of 'the public', include mechanisms for citizen participation, co-operative management, communitarianism and even co-ownership.

Thus the remunicipalization of public services can create the necessary – if not sufficient – conditions for their further democratization, thanks to the smaller scale of the local level. This can be done through the promotion of short supply chains that strengthen the overall community and economic fabric of the municipality. Remunicipalization is understood as a tool for the management of the commons, as citizens organize themselves to provide new services in a democratic and disinterested fashion. This is especially the case when it comes to energy provision.

There are more than 800 documented cases of remunicipalization over the world, involving 1,600 cities and 45 countries, most of them European. The results of this activity are clear, and positive. There are, however, still many tasks and challenges that need to be faced, including the following:

- **The need to adjust legal and institutional frameworks in order to make it easier to implement them.** It is no longer simply a case of there being a legislative system willing to turn a blind eye to things it considers odd. Rather, the system as a whole needs to innovate and promote new ways of managing resources in common. Nation-states, the European Union and international financial organizations are currently more interested in aggressively promoting free trade deals which protect large corporations than in protecting and developing municipal autonomy.
- **Develop networks of local co-operation.** Municipalities often find themselves isolated and alone in the face of opposition when they open the debate about whether to remunicipalize a particular service. This is why the networks of co-operation and mutual learning that exist between municipalities need to be strengthened. Although each case is unique, specific and unrepeatable, the aims, methods and

experiences of others who are working in the same area are vital tools that can help us obtain good results.

- **Experiment with the common wealth.** Remunicipalization is not planned as a way of returning to how things were 20, 30 or 50 years ago. It is a new approach with new practices, new divisions of power and new objectives. It is a field that requires a great deal of trial and error, without any absolute or preconceived ideas of truth. And it requires imagination, bravery and collective intelligence.

Mini-manifesto

- **Promote horizontality** in the relationship between the administration and the citizens, as well as among the co-operative networks.
- **Promote transparency** in order to ensure that the task is well controlled and funded, as well as to ensure public access to all available information.
- **Make sure that decisions are taken communally**, to give power to the community and the municipal area itself.
- **Guarantee universality of access** to any given service to all people, irrespective of their socio-economic or legal situation.

Examples

Remunicipalization of water and electricity services, Paris and Grenoble

Given the mass wave of privatizations that took place in France in the 1980s in the energy sector, most cities and towns in France have spent much of the last few years engaged in trying to regain public control of the water supply.

Paris remunicipalized its water supply in 2010. The reasons that it decided to do this were unhappiness with how the private companies were running the situation, lack of transparency, and a chaotic administrative structure. The first year back in public hands, the water supply made a profit of 35 million euros, which were not distributed to shareholders but which were rather reinvested in the system itself, and the cost of water fell by 8 per cent. A citizens' group was created to observe the management of the water supply: this included representatives of the city's residents' associations, in order to increase the level of public participation in the decision-making process. Agreements were reached with the farmers who work upstream along the Seine for them to use environmentally friendly pesticides, which improved the quality of water reaching the city's taps.

Given the political impact of this remunicipalization process, Paris and other cities such as Brussels and Milan founded the group Aqua Publica Europea.

Grenoble, with its 160,000 inhabitants, was a pioneer in the remunicipalization of the water supply, which it carried out back in 2000. The Grenoble model is now used in various municipalities. Intermunicipal sanitation facilities have lowered the costs for this service and help constantly to improve the quality of the water that is gathered and the treatment of residues, at the same time as maintaining the system by which water is delivered to households. The water supply is sustainable, and the water is of excellent quality. Over the last few years the battle to regain control of energy supplies has begun in Grenoble, and it is also a pioneer in the provision and management of municipal school canteens, which aim to offer food that is 100-per-cent organic and local, thanks to their work with local farmers.

Energy transition in Hamburg

In 2009, the city established an energy company that aimed to promote renewable energy and sell electricity to the network. After only a few years, more than 100,000 people looking for a local and renewable source of energy had signed up to have their electricity provided by the company, . In parallel to this, the hundred-year concession of energy provision granted to private companies to operate the electricity network came to an end, and, given the refusal of the city council to remunicipalize the service, the people organized and won a referendum in 2013 which forcibly returned control of the electricity network to public hands. This finally took place in 2015 and will be followed by the remunicipalization of the gas companies in the next few years. Thus the city has brought together the different elements of the municipal energy sector and can now carry out in a much more straightforward fashion a policy of energy transition to help fight against climate change.

Referenda for public water
Direct democracy has given the struggle for public control of the water supply its greatest ally. In 2004, a constitutional referendum in Uruguay safeguarded public control throughout the country (this is now a model that has been deployed throughout the world); in 2011, 27 million Italians voted 'no' to the marketization of the water supply, a vote which stopped many privatization processes that were at the time under way; in 2013 a popular referendum in Berlin managed to gather 600,000 signatures to make public the contracts by which control of the city's water supply had been granted to private firms: this led to the remunicipalization of the service; in Madrid a popular consultation dealt a severe blow to any plans that were in place for privatizing the city's water supply.

Remunicipalization can only be developed and understood when it happens alongside direct participation and public empowerment.

Feminizing politics
Deconstructing the myth of 'technical questions'
The remunicipalization of public services implies a return of many aspects of public life to the level that is closest to the public, that of the municipality. This creates a sense of proximity that cuts down the distance between those who are providing the service and those who are using it, fusing the roles as much as possible and making the service more democratic. And it is here that we seek a feminization of public services, so that they stop being perceived as a technical matter beyond the reach of the public at large, and become merely one more aspect of daily life.

Working as a global network
Energy Cities
Energy Cities is a network of cities that has been working in Europe for energy transition for over 25 years. Its philosophy is summed up in the idea of the 'three Ds': democratization of the energy system; decentralization of power, bringing it down to a more human level; and diversification, reprioritizing local economic resources. It is a network that offers support and help to all cities that ask for it, which is a great help not just for those cities that are already entering into the process of development and change, but also for those that do not have strong political majorities, and that need the support and assistance of a global brand.

Aqua Publica Europea
Aqua Publica Europea (APE) is the European Association of Public Water Providers, a European network of cities in favour of a publicly owned water supply that offers mutual support in order to provide an ever-improving service. APE brings together public water and sanitation services, along with other parties who work for the public provision of water at a European and international level.

Key concepts
Remunicipalization: In general terms, this is the process by which a local service that had been privatized is taken back into the hands of the town or city council. The ways by which this happens can be very varied: a company might have left public control and later returned to it; the service might have remained in public hands but not the management of it, leading to a situation in which control was *de facto* lost along with information about how the service was being managed; there are even cases in which an entirely new service has been created, such as the establishment in France of new public-community partnerships between councils and farmers in order to supply school canteens. This last case might more accurately be deemed one of 'municipalization'.

Tools and resources

Fearless Cities roundtable: 'Remunicipalization'
youtu.be/rCeiOI7S3Qs

Remunicipalization: How cities and citizens are rewriting the future of public services Satoko Kishimoto, Olivier Petitjean, and Lavinia Steinfort. Transnational Institute, 2017
nin.tl/remunicipalization

17

Transparency and the fight against corruption

Fèlix Beltran (Barcelona En Comú), **Anxela Iglesias García** (Communications Adviser, Madrid City Council) and **Jordi Molina** (Participation and Transparency Adviser, Barcelona City Council)

Democracy is basically the public keeping watch over its own institutions, which is why we need transparency in order to have democracy, because without information we are not conscious and if we are not conscious we can't take decisions or keep watch over anything.

Simona Levi, Xnet

This is not a Puerto Rico struggle. If capital is organized internationally – and it is organized, and very well – as well as controlling the public infrastructure by sponsoring legislation, then we have to organize internationally as well.

Xiomara Caro, Director, New Mobilization Projects, Center for Popular Democracy, US

Context

Corruption is a tumour that affects the common good, and that generates privileges for the few, increases inequality and wastes public resources, generating huge costs for the public purse. Citizens have a right to good government – that is to say, to receive public services that are efficient and transparent. Public resources are a common good, and their redistribution should be transparent, equitable and fair. The contracts for goods, services and public works that local governments can award are a key tool in the distribution of opportunities, and should therefore be based on criteria that are clear and strict. From all sides, but especially at the municipal level, we should demand and promote transparency, and fight against corrupt practices and systems: these are actions that promote equality for all.

Transparency should be a goal for all institutions, and also a medium by which citizens can participate in the democratic process. Although decision-making is in theory put into the hands of the people who live in cities, without information and clear rules it is not possible to truly decide. Increased transparency is a prerequisite for radical democracy.

In the current situation, corruption finds itself more and more often in the hands of criminal organizations operating at an international level, which is why we need to establish institutional and citizen networks to complement existing anti-corruption organizations: we need organized counter-corruption powers and local administrations that are willing to be examples in the fight for transparency at the municipal level, taking into account the peculiarities of each context.

The establishment of a political culture based on values such as co-operation, direct participation and accountability is fundamental in the fight against corruption. Without a change in behaviour on the part of public administrations, political parties and companies, there is no chance of success. But without the involvement of a public that demands higher standards when it comes to making decisions and managing public resources there is no chance of success either.

It is civil society (organized via entities and individual professionals fighting for transparency) and political parties that need to be the leaders in the fight against corruption. One of our challenges is to make sure that public institutions collaborate with these civil-society bodies, and that they work together to create innovative tools and procedures that are open and straightforward. They must be permanently accountable. Internal controls that come from the government itself (public policy decisions or finance legislation, for example) are just as important as those that come from outside, from civil society. We have to keep our eyes on public powers; we have to be alert; we have to organize ourselves; we have to create collective spaces in the struggle against individual interests and opaque practices.

Mini-manifesto

- **Promote a new culture in the process of awarding municipal contracts**, one that promotes a wider bidding pool and greater transparency in public contracts, and which places emphasis on the introduction of gender and social perspectives.
- **Establish ethical codes of conduct for political representatives**, with sanctions available and ethics committees that make sure the codes are fulfilled.
- **Limit mandates for elected officials** and forbid them from leaving their job and moving into lucrative non-governmental activities, in order to make sure that public officials can't use their position to support particular companies and vice versa.
- **Create a public body to combat municipal corruption,** which can receive anonymous denunciations from citizens and municipal figures and can also convene groups to investigate them.
- **Audit municipal debt and expenses**, especially those deriving from the sale of public contracts.
- **Regulate conflicts of interest and incompatible activities**: forbid unjustified travel and gifts that are not consistent with protocol, end the practice of giving grants without an application process, and force elected individuals to declare their interests and activities.
- **Use impact assessment tools** developed by competent officials to make the organization efficient and accountable.
- **Encourage civic and citizen opposition movements** – an organized society that is vigilant and alert to possible cases of corruption. It also needs to be clear that members of these movements will not be adversely affected if they make denunciations of corruption.

Examples

Municipal citizen audit of debt and public policy, Madrid

The municipal debt of Madrid had risen from 1,136 million euros in 2002 to 6,732 million euros in 2015, when the municipalist platform took over the local government.

In order to gather and distribute information on the use of public municipal resources, as well as to analyse the use of municipal funds against criteria of public utility and to arrive at conclusions that would avoid the future repetition of any poor practice that was discovered, the Madrid local government put into action in August 2015 a series of studies, which it called the Municipal citizen audit of debt and public policy, whose objective was the identification and analysis of the ecological, social, economic and gender-related impact of municipal policies.

Using this tool, the Madrid local government also investigated the awarding of public contracts, and incorporated social clauses into the process for awarding public contracts in January 2016, in order to prioritize companies that fulfil various criteria to do with working practices, sustainability, gender and environmental issues. In December 2017 the creation of a Register of Lobbies took place, after having first been mooted in the Madrid Transparency Order of July 2016.

Anti-Corruption Complaint Box, Barcelona City Council with Xnet

After the 2015 elections, one of Barcelona City Council's priorities was to guarantee ethical behaviour and support transparency and the struggle against institutional corruption within its own departments. This was the reason for the creation of the Office of Transparency and Good Practice, which would later become the operations centre from which tools such as the Code of Conduct and the Anti-Corruption Complaint Box would be launched. The latter was an inbox that allowed individuals to communicate anonymously to the Council incidents and forms of behaviour that were contrary to ethical practice. It was made available to elected officials and municipal workers. If, once a denunciation had been received and analysed, it was thought that it showed evidence of illicit practices, then the Office of Transparency and Good Practice would get in touch with the Finance Ministry or the relevant judicial authorities, and pass all the relevant documentation over to them.

This tool was created by Xnet activists. Xnet is a group that works on technopolitics and participation tools, as well as transparency and citizen control of the reins of power. Xnet has worked disinterestedly with local government in making this tool. The close collaboration of the two has allowed Xnet to develop codes and protocols that make the Anti-Corruption Complaint Box internationally the first of its kind in the institutional sphere. Also, as it was built using shareware and open code, it is easy for other administrations to adopt and adapt the Complaint Box for their needs. The Catalonia and Valencia anti-fraud offices have incorporated this technology into their work, free of charge, and it is expected that other offices will join the initiative.

Feminizing politics

Transparency, and the struggle against corruption, is key to the feminization or de-patriarchalization of politics. Various global studies conclude that the population as a whole perceives women as less corrupt and more honest, although this clearly depends on the political context (whether the country is more democratic and transparent, or more autocratic): this is especially true in the case of bribery and administrative irregularities. This is a situation that can be explained by gender socialization (women are given less incentive to transgress the norms), and also because women do not traditionally have access to informal and social 'male' spaces, where such corrupt deals are usually prepared. This is another argument in favour of a greater feminization of politics.

Also, a public contracts policy that looks to address gender and social imbalances is particularly important for jobs in the care industry, which are normally contracted out, insecure and mainly occupied by women.

Key concepts

Citizen debt audit: This is an initiative promoted by citizens' groups to audit the public accounts of administrations and determine which elements of the income and expenditure, and the public debt that these generate, are illegitimate, in order to compel local government organs not to pay it, as well as to put the individuals responsible for such illegitimate spending through a suitable legal process. Amongst other benefits, this process strengthens the transparency of the local government's economic activity, which allows local government to become more democratic, as it enlarges the framework within which information is disseminated and citizen participation is sought. It also makes the government more effective, as it helps avoid cases of misuse of public funds and poor public policy.

Tools and resources

Fearless Cities roundtable: 'Transparency and the fight against corruption'
nin.tl/transparency

Committee for the Abolition of Illegitimate Debt
cadtm.org/English

Municipal Citizens' Observatory
ocmunicipal.net/en/

18

Economies for the common good

Tánia Corrons (Barcelona En Comú), **Isabel Álvarez** (Municipal Research and Support Network – Redinam) and **David Fernández** (Researcher in Development and Regional Innovation)

The transformation we seek is to generate an economy which serves the people, by which I don't mean the financiers who have up until now decided on the economy's focus, but rather the people themselves.
Susana Martín, Social Monetary Institute

Context

The politics of local economic development have traditionally run along two lines: policies aimed at attracting the global economic actors, which very regularly involve creating special local conditions in order to attract large companies; and policies aimed at transforming local initiatives into global or international phenomena. Municipalism proposes a third approach, that of internally focused local development, which values pre-existing local resources and seeks to satisfy the needs of citizens with these resources, at city, district, suburb or village level; and which incorporates a number of perspectives, including those of transition and dynamic processes.

Any policy of internally focused local development has to include the externalities it gives rise to, such as its effects on the surrounding environment and on reproductive labour, and to reduce any negative impact by focusing on companies that are small, with a variety of ways of engaging with the public, and that are local, rooted in particular areas of a city, and possessing well-defined social and environmental aims that lie beyond pure economic gain. Cities with more local development have less inequality, healthier citizens, more social capital, more diversity; the companies based there have more of an interest in the development of the wider community.

In order to achieve these objectives, municipal areas that opt for economic policies that contribute to the common good create many and varied tools. These share a few common denominators, which will be described below.

Mini-manifesto

Co-produce economic policy with local people, creating local development campaigns at the district or neighbourhood level, and even looking beyond the physical boundaries of the municipal area, following the logic of joint action between society and the local administration.

Provide incentives for the Social and Solidarity Economy (SSE) and the circular economy. In order to promote the SSE it is vital to focus on socio-economic innovation as well as the role of the public sector. Socio-economic innovation consists in innovations which may be technological, social or environmental, but which all have a social mission, connected to the needs of the local population. It is vital to generate services, resources and tools that can help the development of the social economy – not to be a substitute for public services, but rather to complement them. It is also necessary to generate dense productive structures that can draw from differently sized companies and research institutes.

Support innovative local technologies that can strengthen the local economic and social fabric. An interesting example of such tools is the idea of local currency. Taking advantage of new technologies, a chance has arisen to democratize the monetary-finance system. Social currencies contribute to local development for various reasons: they can help lessen the impact of monetary crises and avoid the collapse of local economies; they can promote local consumption, for they create additional income which has to be spent at the local level, usually on food; when public projects are financed with local currencies, the money can't flee to global interests, which strengthens the local economy; they allow value to be created at a local level for local projects, which means that it can't be taken away to finance the projects of big capital.

Use responsible procurement to promote the democratization of business. Tools that exist at the municipal level, such as codes of responsible conduct for contract providers – which prioritize criteria such as social inclusion and gender equality in the workplace, or the creation of stable jobs with fair salaries – or else the creation of bodies that promote social dialogue, can all help spread the democratic business impulse beyond the standard participants in the SSE, and reach the 'traditional' private sector.

Examples

MARES, Madrid

Via projects promoted by the SSE, citizens can discover new ways of resolving collective problems and develop social-innovation initiatives. The MARES project, which the Madrid local government and various social entities in the city put into action in January 2017, seeks to make the discovery and use of these solutions more powerful. Four zones, in different districts of the city, serve as meeting places and areas where citizen initiatives in five sectors – mobility, food, recycling and energy (the fifth sector is that of the city itself, present in each of the zones) – can be discussed and fleshed out. Among the activities being carried out at the moment are:

- mapping all the SSE initiatives in the city, along with attempts to find possible areas of connection or complementarity between them (the so-called 'chains of value');
- the audit of more than 70 projects;
- the constitution of a co-operative that aims to help small businesses get off the ground;
- the establishment of practice-oriented learning

communities, in which groups of individuals combine their knowledge in order to learn together and start projects based in the local community.

The project also aims to stimulate the capacity for autonomous organization and development of community initiatives in those sectors of the population that are particularly precariously employed.

SSE impulse plan, Barcelona

Barcelona has a powerful fabric of neighbourhood associations: SSE projects, whether or not they were structured as co-operative ventures, were working with thousands of citizen initiatives in 2015, which represented eight per cent of the working population and involved sums equivalent to seven per cent of the city's GDP. The SSE impulse plan aims to reinforce and facilitate access to the SSE and work with the public, and has recruited working groups throughout SSE-affiliated organizations, from the local development agencies to the local authority itself; it has a development budget of four million euros each year. The plan brings together dozens of interrelated actions, such as practical training in different formats and with different objectives, assessment tribunals for people who want to put plans into action, co-operative finance initiatives and microcredit (two million euros), economic support (three million euros annually) and support teams run by local government as well as by the SSE itself (from groups such as El Faro de la Innovación Socioeconòmica or Coopolis). There are also initiatives that aim to integrate these activities at a local level, by for example developing district-based economic plans and so on.

At the time of writing, more than 100 new projects and more than 100 businesses have been advised annually, and more than 1,500 individuals have received training. The municipal government has promoted collective entrepreneurship for vulnerable groups, and has supported initiatives such as the Alencoop scrap-metal collection service. It has also supported the growth of international networks of municipalities and cities that support the SSE, such as CITIESS and the Xarxa de Municipis per l'Economia Social i Solidària (X-MESS).

From the circular economy to the temporary occupation of public spaces, Paris

The municipal government wishes the city to be the world capital of an economy that promotes social innovation and transition to renewable resources. In order to make this happen, there are various municipal plans in place, the most important of which is the following: the development of the circular economy using 240 social agents from Grand Paris, which carry out activities such as:

- the creation of *ressourceries*, a network of sites where unused objects can be recovered, processed and sold;
- the reincorporation of marginalized individuals into the working environment by, for example, insisting on responsible public contracting practices;
- actions such as the temporary occupation of public spaces and public buildings by SSE-affiliates;
- the creation of points where services can be exchanged within the local community.

Some of these measures are now having an impact: Paris gives financial support to seven co-operatives that deal in activism and entrepreneurship, helping to get young people into work; the temporary occupation of public buildings has allowed an artists' association to set up studios throughout the city.

Feminizing politics

The birth and spread of the collaborative economy have presented several challenges from the point of view of gender. Although the SSE is normally by its nature much more open and inclusive than the traditional economy, it still manages in some ways to reflect traditional patterns of gender discrimination. Women do participate in significant numbers in the collaborative sector, but they are more prevalent in areas of production viewed as traditionally feminine. At the same time, there are studies that show how women are more usually present in the sphere of consumption (passive) than in that of production (active), where men usually uphold and reproduce sexist norms. There may be an evident and generalized division of labour in the collaborative economy but, if there is, it is a discrimination against the role of women in collective activities. Also, the number of women in the upper echelons of the government is extremely low.

Part of the problem is related to the limits that a law has when it comes to intervention and guaranteeing a legal framework in which collaborating organizations can operate and protect people from discrimination of all kinds. But there are positive signs for the future, such as increased academic interest in investigating this topic, and institutional programmes that aim to provide real, open and inclusive models for how the collaborative economy might be run in the future.

Working as a global network

Intercontinental Network for the Promotion of the Social Solidarity Economy

The RIPESS (Red Intercontinental de Promoción de la Economía Social Solidaria) is the largest worldwide network of groups that are committed to the SSE. It is both global and local in reach and this grants it legitimacy to promote the SSE, to support international co-operation and to get involved in politics at various different levels. The RIPESS is predisposed to contribute to a systemic and transformative change, and can show clearly how the SSE can provide local-level answers to a dominant system whose limits are all too clear.

Key concepts

Internally focused local economic development: This is economic development that is primarily concerned with proximity, that values existing resources and considers how to satisfy people's needs with these resources.

Tools and resources

Fearless Cities roundtable: 'Economy'
youtu.be/mZkRSpDBFDc

Centre de recherche sur les innovations sociales (CRISES)
This is an interdisciplinary and inter-university organization based at the University of Québec in Montreal, which researches the role of social innovation, understood as activities that have the capacity to transform social relations and set up new cultural focuses.
crises.uqam.ca/presentation

Intercontinental Network for the Promotion of the Social Solidarity Economy (RIPESS)
ripess.org/?lang=en

Cities Building Community Wealth Marjorie Kelly and Sarah McKinley, Democracy Collaborative, 2015
democracycollaborative.org/cities

19

Sanctuary cities

Bue Hansen (Barcelona En Comú), **Anna Rius** (Councillor, Terrassa City Council), **Ignasi Calbó** (Co-ordinator of the Refuge City Plan, Barcelona City Council) and **Céline Gagne** (OMNES, Greece)

Migration is a fundamental freedom that must be defended.
Amélie Canonne, Emmaus International, Paris

Refugee and migration policy must cut across all policy in City Hall, from economic and social policy to urban planning. It should be seen as an asset, not as a problem.
Ignasi Calbó, Co-ordinator of the Refuge City Plan, Barcelona City Council

Context

While national governments build walls and fences, cities and towns are welcoming refugees and providing spaces of sanctuary to undocumented residents. Around the world, cities and towns are challenging the rise of the far right, and local governments and social movements are working to protect human rights and forge inclusive, non-ethnocentric solidarities and communities.

Newcomers have always arrived in cities, and they will continue to arrive. Welcoming is not so much a question of benevolence, but of creating the conditions for conviviality. It's a question of how we can avoid our cities becoming divided by the state's distinction between those who have national citizenship and those who do not.

Municipalism plays a key role in challenging the rise of xenophobia; local governments and social movements can work to enforce human rights and forge inclusive, non-ethnocentric urban citizenship. Municipalism allows us to understand citizenship as something more than 'papers', as referring to everyone who co-inhabits, produces and reproduces the city and its rights.

But the task is far from a simple one. If we want to support newcomers in becoming active co-producers of the right to the city we must find ways of providing refuge and sanctuary that do not turn newcomers into clients or leave them internally excluded. And if we want to go beyond the idea of 'assimilation into the nation', the process of inviting people into our neighbourhoods, movements and institutions must be one that transforms us all.

Unless we embrace the challenge of producing urban citizenship, our cities will be ever more divided. Mistrust, scapegoating and competition for scarce resources will undermine labour solidarity, and support for the commons and universal welfare.

If municipalities, local institutions such as schools and libraries, associations and social movements actively welcome refugees, a great deal can be done locally to build conviviality and counter racist stereotypes. The city is a privileged terrain for the development of post-national subjectivity because it's where tensions around citizenship, exclusion and othering have always played out. Welcoming refugees is not just good for local life, but also for global solidarities, as it undermines the dehumanization, abandonment and exclusion of those who suffer most from a world characterized by inequality, climate change and deadly geopolitics.

Municipal governments and the terrain of municipal politics can play a significant role in strengthening these horizons, practices and networks of solidarity, by affirming openness, providing resources and infrastructure for welcoming, and even practising municipal disobedience.

Mini-manifesto

- **Encourage civic participation** by recognizing migrants' voices, demands and self-organization.

- **Treat migrants as citizens from day one**, by including them in local and municipal democracy (from associations and school boards to public consultations and participatory budgeting).
- **House newcomers among locals**, rather than in camps that stigmatize and isolate them. Any emergency temporary housing must also be open to long-term locals.
- **Give longer-term residents, refugees and migrants equal access to public services, housing and benefits** to avoid a sense of competition, exclusion or preferential treatment, and so that longer-term residents have a stake in the preservation of services that migrants also depend on. On some issues, like language classes or help for people with traumas from war or persecution, there may be a need to provide targeted services, but even these can be combined with publicly subsidized literacy training for locals, taught in the same language schools.
- **Combat institutional racism** by ending or undermining exclusionary and dehumanizing policies and institutions, such as detention centres, refugee camps and 'refugee-only' buildings.
- **Change municipal by-laws and policing** to decriminalize the survival strategies and lifestyles of the poor.
- **Challenge national governments** when they breach or fail to live up to their human rights commitments.
- **Empower immigrants** by providing language courses, working courses, legal aid and advice.
- **Empower civil society and trade unions** as agents of integration into civic life and existing organizations and networks of solidarity.

Examples

Municipal ID cards, New York

Cities are increasingly using municipal ID cards as tools of equity and inclusion. Municipal ID cards reduce barriers for vulnerable groups that traditionally have difficulty obtaining or maintaining government-issued photo identification, such as people experiencing homelessness, survivors of domestic abuse, undocumented immigrants, previously incarcerated persons, transgender and gender non-conforming persons, senior citizens and young people.

New York City is home to one of the world's largest municipal ID programmes – IDNYC – which it launched in 2015. In the specific case of undocumented immigrants, city residents are able to apply for an IDNYC card without reference to immigration status. Cardholders can designate their preferred language on the back of the card, as well as their preferred gender, or no gender, on the front.

IDNYC acts as a powerful tool of inclusion by facilitating access to city services and granting entry to public buildings. For instance, with IDNYC, parents can pick their children up from school and participate confidently in school life, for example through parent-teacher associations. IDNYC can be used in interactions with the New York Police Department, to check into city hospitals, access health and immunization records, open a bank account, access public library resources, and get discounts at hundreds of wellness and cultural institutions. Today, over one million New Yorkers are IDNYC cardholders. A 2016 external assessment of the IDNYC programme found that 77 per cent of immigrant users reported that having an IDNYC card increased their sense of belonging in the city.

OMNES, Kilkis, Greece

OMNES ('all' in Latin), started in Kilkis, northern Greece, in response to the many refugees and migrants who were stranded there when the Balkan route to northern Europe was closed. Working from the principle that everyone in need should have independent and dignified housing and be included in the community, OMNES decided to work for housing solutions that would not only target people seeking international protection. Currently, it hosts more than 500 people in 115 rented apartments. Among them are local families facing homelessness, and individuals and families who are seeking or have obtained refugee or subsidiary protection status. OMNES supports solidarity economy initiatives and seeks to strengthen people's access to public services for all by informing them about their social rights. The association also works to improve public services by transforming centralized programmes that treat people as passive clients, or replacing them with initiatives that promote ownership, local contextualization, participation and proximity.

The Trampoline House, Copenhagen, Denmark
The Trampoline House was started by a group of socially engaged artists, who visited an isolated camp for asylum-seekers outside Copenhagen. Their aim was to ask the residents of the camp what they might be able to do together. Out of this dialogue came a social centre in Copenhagen, an urban base that could break the rural isolation of the camp. The house, which is supported by municipal funding, has given newcomers and locals a space for social, economic and learning activities, from language classes and language exchanges, to parties, debates and film screenings, from a hairdressing salon to a catering co-operative. The Trampoline House is run in a horizontal and participative way, in which everyone is treated as a co-citizen from day one. The basic idea is that the house functions as a centre of democratic training, for both newcomers and long-term residents, teaching both groups to act democratically together in their everyday lives. The results are very clear: those who pass through the house have an easier time accessing jobs, learning Danish and developing social relations in their new country, and the house produces an all-too-rare space for social interaction between newcomers and locals.

Repopulating a shrinking village with refugees, Riace, Italy
Fifteen years ago, the hilltop medieval village of Riace on Italy's south coast was almost a ghost town, with derelict houses and the local school on the verge of closure. The village was in danger of disappearing as residents moved to northern Italy and elsewhere searching for jobs. Riace changed its destiny by openly welcoming refugees to live and work as part of the community. This transformation was instigated by the

mayor, Domenico Lucano, who set up a scheme, funded by the Italian government, to offer refugees abandoned apartments and provide training. The initiative has rebuilt the economy and population; about 450 migrants, drawn from 20 countries beyond Europe, now live in Riace, making up about a quarter of the village's population.

Feminizing politics

Women make up more than 50 per cent of the world's inhabitants, and non-white people make up an even larger part. Cities of sanctuary and refuge try to develop alternatives to the systematic devaluation of non-white life, as well as the systematic exploitation of non-citizens and their exclusion from formal political participation. Migrant women are in danger of becoming invisible as well as facing a double oppression as women and as migrants, and it must be a priority to empower their self-organization as well as to focus attention on the violence suffered during the migratory process. Cities must work to enable women to be economically self-sufficient and must also confront the lack of working rights given by the state, so that family life becomes a choice rather than a necessity.

Feminist and anti-racist politics are not merely questions of ethics, but of strategy. Transformatory politics will be weak unless it finds ways to build solidarity across constructed divisions, ways to undermine competition and resentment based on gender, citizenship status and ethnicity.

Working as a global network

Solidarity Cities

Solidarity Cities is an initiative of the EUROCITIES network and was launched in 2016 in response to the migration crisis. Driven by Barcelona, Athens, Berlin and Amsterdam, Solidarity Cities aims to highlight the political leadership of cities in managing migration. Its work is structured around four pillars:

• Exchange of information and knowledge on the refugee situation in cities

- Advocacy for increased involvement and direct funding for cities in welcoming refugees
- City-to-city technical and financial assistance and capacity-building
- Eliciting pledges by European cities to receive relocated asylum-seekers.

One of Solidarity Cities' main demands is for cities to have the ability to relocate refugees between them directly on the basis of their capacity to host them, without the authorization of national governments. An attempt by Barcelona to take in 100 refugees directly from Athens was blocked by the Spanish central government in March 2016.

Key concepts

Solidarity: In contrast to charity, solidarity refers to the recognition of common interests and common struggles, and to the need to abolish rather than ameliorate and maintain inequalities.

Urban citizenship: As opposed to national citizenship, which divides the inhabitants of the city according to the 'legality' of their presence, urban citizenship belongs to everyone who lives in, produces and reproduces a city. It refers to the shared interest in co-inhabitation based on equality, conviviality and mutual respect. It acknowledges that those who do not have the right to vote are also capable of demanding and producing rights through their political agency.

'For all': Rights to housing, benefits, education, etc, must be universal as far as possible, to avoid both the exclusion of migrants through racism and impressions of migrants receiving preferential treatment, which can be used to fuel racism.

Tools and resources

Fearless Cities policy roundtable: 'Sanctuary cities'
youtu.be/g4Z0VdFWgQ4

'Refugees welcome'   Speech by Ada Colau, 4 September 2015
youtube.com/watch?v=9iVLXQOV1bo

'We, the cities of Europe', Open letter, 13 September 2015
nin.tl/openletter

'Don't make us ashamed of being Europeans'
Open letter by Ada Colau, Mayor of Barcelona; Giuseppina
Nicoli, Mayor of Lampedusa; and Spyros Galinos, Mayor of
Lesbos, 16 March 2016
nin.tl/Colauetal

Epilogue: Transforming fear into hope

Ada Colau, Mayor of Barcelona

As a consequence of the brutal neoliberalism that has managed to take hold of the global economic system, we live in a world in which inequalities and injustice are increasing at an alarming rate. In a world like this, the future has become an uncertain place for millions of people.

This means that more and more people are living in fear: in fear of losing their job, their home, their pension or even their life at the hands of an abusive partner or in a terrorist attack. It is a fear which at its deepest level can be expressed by four words: fear of the Other.

Neofascism, the far-right movement that is growing in Europe, takes advantage of this fear by pointing to this 'Other' as the cause of all ills. They want to create a division between 'us', the good guys, the ones who have always been here, and 'them', the unknown, the ones who threaten everything we have left, the ones who are 'not like us'.

We have witnessed, dumbstruck, the Brexit referendum result, the election of Donald Trump, and the tragedy of millions of refugees barely surviving or dying 'with nowhere to go'. These phenomena are the fruits of fear, and must be defeated.

But in order to defeat them, we must first understand them. Fear is a legitimate emotion. Globalization has brought us together, has made everyone realize that we are all connected, but it has also made us feel more alone, and more insignificant, than ever.

The current economic system only increases social inequality and has created a division between those at the top, the 'winners', and those at the bottom, who are shamelessly dubbed the 'losers'.

The far right is nothing more than a response to the social unease generated by this division. But it is a dangerous response, even though many people find it a tempting one, as it allows them to swap the people 'at the top' for 'our people', or the people 'from here', and set them against 'the others', the strangers, the ones who 'come over here' to take what is ours. But this kind of essentialism, this exclusive nationalism and xenophobia can never be an answer to anything. Quite the opposite.

Both divisions – 'above/below', 'us/the others' – are reductive and dangerous: they do nothing other than increase the level of fear in the world and put at risk the democratic rights and freedoms which it took our grandparents so much effort to achieve. Municipalism seeks to do away with these divisions, starting from the place where we all recognize one another as equals: the community. Our neighbourhoods, our towns, our cities. Municipalism is an emerging force that seeks to transform fear into hope from the bottom up, and to build this hope together, in common.

We began our municipalist adventure having been inspired by struggles against the cutbacks to rights following the economic crisis: the struggle against evictions, against the dismantling of the education system, against the cuts to healthcare and the public sector in general. For years we challenged from the streets a system that had 'legalized' vast injustices. These struggles united us and taught us that together we were stronger in the face of the greed of speculators and a public administration that protected the privileges of a few instead of defending the rights of the many.

We set out on this adventure simultaneously in many different cities. And if we won elections, it was because we knew that we were not alone, that the experience of people in Madrid was the same as ours. And the experience of people in Zaragoza, in Valencia, in A Coruña, in Iruña, in Cádiz, in Santiago de Compostela. And in Valparaíso in Chile, in Jackson, Mississippi, in Grenoble in France, and in so many other countries, from Italy to Poland.

The first Fearless Cities summit was held in Barcelona in June 2017 to celebrate the force of municipalism that unites us.

I remember that during the event I, as mayor of Barcelona, felt greatly honoured to see so many people who had come from so far away, from so many different cities, from so many countries, from every continent, in order to share their ideas, suggestions and concerns. I like to believe that it was not by chance that this first municipalist gathering took place in our city: Barcelona has always been brave, open, innovative, supportive and progressive. A pioneering city in the defence of rights and freedoms.

The marvellous thing about what happened in Barcelona over those days is that the meeting was far more than a simple summit. It was a public proclamation, a cry to the heavens that we wanted, together, to move towards a better future. In a brave, united voice, we said loud and clear that we wanted to change the world, working at the local level through concrete actions and policies that not only improve people's lives, but also show that there is an alternative, and that politics should work for the many and put people at the centre.

It was there that we realized we were taking a huge step forwards with something that is essential to our project: we needed to collaborate as a network. The phrase 'globalizing municipalism' may sound slightly contradictory, but it is not. It is simply a way of overcoming the divisions between 'above and below', 'us and the others' in order to create an international network of cities that defend human rights, that fight together against climate change and misogyny and against all the policies that only benefit a few and condemn the rest to uncertainty and fear.

Together, we want to stop the far right, end violent extremism and stop the pushback that we are seeing against civil rights and liberties.

Now that we have found each other, our challenge is to make cities into a real and concrete alternative, based in the local sphere and community, and by feminizing politics. An alternative that builds a fairer world, a society without the fractures that serve the interests of those who don't want change because they don't want to lose their privileges. A society of rights and opportunities for all.

For some years now, in municipal areas all over the world, we have been experimenting with something new: people who had never governed a city, who had done politics from social movements, NGOs or neighbourhood associations, are now inside municipal institutions. And we are building bridges between municipal politics and new forms of political action by citizens from different walks of life to defy an established order that is profoundly unjust.

Our goal is to find one another, to make sure everyone in society can have the same opportunity for influence, in the same way, transparent and democratic, on the decisions of the government. Our goal is also to stand up, when necessary, to the abuses of the economic and financial elites. Because we outnumber them – and the more of us who are involved the better.

Democracy is a word that needs to be reclaimed because, for years, it has been emptied of its original meaning from above. That is why we, in our profound conviction that power belongs to the people, are co-producing public policy in the most democratic way possible, in order to make sure that measures are not just imposed from the top down, but can also be proposed from the bottom up.

Each day that passes, municipalism is weaving its own international web of solidarity. I am convinced that this book, *Fearless Cities: A Guide To the Global Municipalist Movement*, will help spread the spirit and the practices of this great international family. It is up to us to work together to increase the horizon of the possible.

GLOBAL MUNICIPALIST MAP

A directory of **50 municipalist organizations** from 19 countries on every continent. The organizations featured have been selected based on their active collaboration with Barcelona En Comú and with one another.

Fearless Cities

1 Ahora Madrid
2 Aranzadi - Pamplona En Común
3 Arsave - Laboratorio per la cittá che vogliamo
4 Autrement pour Saillans
5 Bancada Ativista
6 Barcelona En Comú
7 Beirut Madinati
8 Buongiorno Livorno

9 Cambiamo Messina dal Basso
10 Cidadâos Por Lisboa
11 Ciudad Futura
12 Coalizione Civica per Bologna
13 Coalizione Civica per Padova
14 Compostela Aberta
15 Comú de Lleida
16 Cooperation Jackson
17 Crida per Sabadell

18 CUP de Celrà - Poble Actiu
19 Decide Roma
20 Demokratik Toplum Kongresi
21 Demosistō
22 Guanyem Badalona en Comú
23 Halklarin Demokratik Partisi
24 Independents for Frome

Ahora Madrid
Madrid Now

ahoramadrid.org

Madrid, Spain

Ahora Madrid arose from the capacity we all have to face up to things we don't like, in order to create, using our imagination and strength, new things in their place. We are helping to create institutions worthy of the citizens who have spent years showing that they are superior to political parties, and that they can solve for themselves the political problems of the city that institutions don't want to deal with.

After more than 20 years of government by the conservative Partido Popular, Madrid has decided to opt for change. The citizens of Madrid demanded change and government that was more honest, transparent, democratic and participatory; a government that is concerned with what people really need. They need new solutions to the social emergencies that shake the city. They need a government that puts people first. They need people who look at the future of the city with no qualms, in order to face up to the challenges it offers decisively and realistically.

Because of this, it was the organized citizens' group that won the Madrid municipal elections in 2015 and that is curing the city day by day. This is a project that is made up of many different people, who collaborate to define their political programme. It was founded through the collective work of Ganemos Madrid ('Let's Win Madrid'), a political movement which promotes democratic municipalism and which enjoys the participation of individuals from various social movements, collectives and parties; and by agreement with Podemos, a political party which wants to win back political institutions for the people. A diverse list of candidates came into office and has formed the Team for Change that runs Madrid today. The Co-ordination Table is our organizational body; it takes important decisions and meets as necessary. The Municipal Group follows the actions of the government. This is a political project that is owned by its members, from the councillors all the way to the people who participate at a local level or in the various thematic Ahora groups.

We want institutions that are close to the people. We support a local government that is everybody's home. A local government that is open, a space where we can debate, make suggestions and participate. There are other ways to manage Madrid, and we count on you to help us find them. Because the most important aspect of leadership is being ready to listen.

Aranzadi – Pamplona En Común

Aranzadi – Pamplona in Common

aranzadi2015.info
Pamplona, Spain

Aranzadi – Pamplona En Común is a municipalist platform that was started by activists from various social movements in Pamplona in the autumn of 2014. The new political space that the 15M demonstrations had opened up made it possible to dream of a change of government in Iruñea [the Basque name for Pamplona] after 30 years of rightwing control.

After an unsuccessful attempt to form a wider coalition, the method chosen to present our candidacy at the 2015 municipal elections was that of presenting 'citizen candidates', each of whom needed to gather 5,000 signatures to be allowed to stand: it was this effort that gave them their initial opportunity to meet the people in their neighbourhoods face to face, in order to develop an electoral plan that was put together via an open and participative process.

In parallel with this, Aranzadi – Pamplona En Común drew up a code of ethics and began a process of open primaries that led to the creation of an open and diverse list of candidates. This won the backing of Podemos and EQUO [the Spanish Green Party]. Aranzadi won almost 10,000 votes in the municipal elections of May 2015: this gained them three posts on the city council and they helped form a government for change with the support of three other political groups: EH Bildu, Geroa Bai and IE. After drawing up a programmatic agreement, Aranzadi joined a council led by Joseba Asirón of EH Bildu, and was given the responsibility for three offices of the council.

The campaign slogan that Aranzadi used was 'Govern by listening', and this has been the method which we have used in this collective experience of learning to govern ourselves. Decisions have been taken in assembly, and for the most important questions (the pact with the government, or the programmatic agreement) we have used online surveys to gather opinion.

Aranzadi's work in the Pamplona council has been fundamental in getting decisions taken about such topics as sustainable public transport, energy autonomy (along with an ambitious plan for commercializing the municipal energy supply), historical memory, and the rejection of touristification. We have also made topics such as male-female equality, violence against women, and LGBTI rights central to our political ideas. Dozens of participative groupings, the creation and consolidation of several autonomous community centres that work alongside the city council, along with squatters' initiatives, have all created a network of self-governing spaces such as Iruñea has never seen before today. This, alongside other tools such as Zentro, the School of Empowerment, is laying the foundations for a culture of participation which will help us build, from the ground up, a city that is more social, more feminist and more sustainable, and whose wealth is much more fairly distributed.

Arsave – Laboratorio per la città che vogliamo
Arsave – Lab for the city that we want

laboratorioarsave.wordpress.com
Reggio Emilia, Emilia Romagna, Italy

Arsave* – Laboratorio per la città che vogliamo is a political collective committed to building a municipalist platform in Reggio Emilia. With origins in the Laboratorio No Expo initiative, the platform was launched in the autumn of 2015 by activists from a range of social movements and associations, civic committees and individual citizens. Arsave is engaged in a process to radically change the city government through citizen involvement in public life and decisions regarding the city's community.

Arsave's political priorities are: restoring and building local democracy; defending the commons and creating 'common' institutions; universal access to public goods; promoting the civic and collective use of public space in the interests of mutualism and solidarity; fighting uncontrolled construction and gentrification; combating the degradation of the local environment; preventing the privatization of public services; remunicipalizing the city's water company and the other privatized public services; opposing securitization and ensuring inclusive policies for refugees and migrants, and reducing poverty, marginalization and social disintegration.

Arsave aims to promote a 'civic coalition' bringing together members of local movements, associations and parties, and ordinary people around a shared municipalist platform to stand in local elections.

Arsave is co-operating with Università Invisibile, an informal project that seeks to develop and share knowledge useful in local movements and institutional action.

For Arsave, feminism and the feminization of politics are essential to promote women's perspectives and involvement

---

* Arsave means 'language in reverse'. It was used by Officine Reggiane workers and the Santa Croce partisan community during the fascist period.

(in both formal representation and informal participation) and to support democratic practices such as horizontal working methods, consensus-seeking, empathy and co-operation, and collective leadership.

Autrement pour Saillans
Differently for Saillans

Saillans, France

Autrement pour Saillans is a citizen platform formed by residents of the municipality concerned for the future of Saillans, a village of 1,251 inhabitants located in the department of Drôme. In the local elections of 2014, Autrement ran on a platform of co-constructing a new mode of collegial and participatory local governance. Its election slogan was 'No programme, no candidates: you're on the ballot paper!' Autrement won 12 of the 15 seats on the city council, with voter turnout rising to a record-breaking 80 per cent.

Autrement's elected representatives have transformed what was a hierarchical government structure in order to work on a collegial basis, sharing power and taking decisions collectively. This method is based on four pillars:

- A division of powers and salaries between all elected representatives, including those of the opposition, with the goal of involving and empowering them all and recognizing their contributions.
- Work is assigned to teams of two or three councillors with the goal of enriching debates, taking decisions collectively and sharing responsibilities.
- The government has replaced the traditional local council with a Steering Committee open to the public and held every two weeks. This is the village's main site of decision-making.

Residents of Saillans can participate in local politics in two main ways:

- Thematic participatory committees: each of these seven committees is co-ordinated by a pair of elected representatives.

They aim to be a space for debate and reflection where main policy positions are defined and specific actions are prioritized. Any resident interested in the issues of the committee can participate.

- Action-project groups: these groups prepare, monitor and implement municipal policies and initiatives defined by the thematic committees. Each group is made up of at least one elected representative and a number of residents, and has a life-span defined by the policies it is responsible for.

In Autrement's first year in government, 230 people (24 per cent of the adult population) took part in the committees and action-project groups.

Bancada Ativista
Activist Bench

bancadaativista.org
São Paulo, Brazil

Bancada Ativista is a non-party movement of citizens from the city and province of São Paulo, which supports many social, economic, political and environmental causes, and which seeks to bring activists to power in legislative bodies at all levels of the Brazilian Federation. It was organized in order to restore the confidence of citizens in politics as a way of transforming reality by occupying the streets, squares and institutions of the city. It promotes an idea of politics which is focused on the individual and which is connected to real questions of our lives and our bodies. It was founded to coincide with the municipal elections of 2016 and has based its practice on the idea of 'learning by doing'. Bancada Ativista supports the candidacies of activists from underrepresented groups, who have never held elected office, and who share their visions of the world and of practical policies.

Bancada Ativista seeks to revive institutional politics and promote its principles and practices via a collaborative and educative approach to electioneering, escaping the corrupt

157

practices of traditional politics. Its fundamental principles are as follows: the unfettered promotion of human rights; the fight against social and economic inequality in policy decisions, and the creation of a city that is collective, human, diverse and which supports its citizens and its public spaces. Bancada Ativista has a few immoveable foundations: openness, transparency and citizen participation.

Barcelona En Comú
Barcelona In Common

barcelonaencomu.cat
Barcelona, Spain

Barcelona En Comú is a municipalist platform launched in Barcelona in June 2014 by activists from a range of social movements. Barcelona En Comú's manifesto was drawn up through citizen participation and its policy priorities include radicalizing democracy, stopping evictions, fighting touristification, remunicipalizing the city's water company, and reducing economic inequalities between neighbourhoods. The organization won the May 2015 city elections, forming a minority government under the leadership of mayor and former housing rights activist Ada Colau.

Barcelona En Comú is structured as a 'confluence', meaning that it brings together ordinary people and members of local political movements and parties in a new project that puts shared goals above partisan interests. According to this philosophy, activists in Barcelona En Comú participate as individuals, rather than in the name of any party or group they may belong to.

Barcelona En Comú is based on collective learning-by-doing rather than abstract theories of change. It seeks to achieve small victories that demonstrate that change is possible and that serve to engage more people to work towards even greater change. One of its first steps was to crowd-source a code of ethics for its elected representatives that limits their salaries and terms in office, and subjects them to strict transparency requirements.

Feminism is at the heart of Barcelona En Comú's municipalism. The organization uses mechanisms to ensure gender parity in both formal representation (electoral lists and governing bodies) and informal participation (speaking time in assemblies). It also seeks to feminize politics; that is, to promote values and practices that have been traditionally undervalued in political life, including consensus-seeking, empathy and co-operation, non-academic expertise, collective leadership and care work.

Beirut Madinati
Beirut My City

beirutmadinati.com
Beirut, Lebanon

Beirut Madinati is a local political platform that was conceived by activists and experts of the city with the goal of taking their commitment and their hard work to the next level. Its work started in 2016, when Beirut Madinati ran for the municipal elections, winning around 40 per cent of the vote against a list of all the traditional parties in Lebanon.

The platform came together with the desire to improve Beirut: its public spaces, mobility, air quality, affordability, waste management, basic services and governance.

Beirut Madinati aims to provide an alternative, starting from local politics and outside of sectarian and private interests. The platform is committed to being inclusive and participatory, putting transparency and accountability at the forefront of its values. It aims to ensure human equality and social justice and reclaim human, economic and political rights. It also aspires to preserve the cultural and natural heritage of Beirut.

Today, Beirut Madinati comprises three main working groups:
• The **Alternative Municipality of Beirut** in Beirut Madinati seeks to bring together its members and its supporters in a collective process of deliberation, advocacy, lobbying, and visioning that influences the future of Beirut positively. It

seeks to set the agenda and prioritize the interests of city residents in the formulation of urban policy.

- The **Elections Working Group** seeks to build on the successes achieved by Beirut Madinati in the 2016 municipal elections, particularly in laying out the groundwork and allocating the required resources to improve the city dwellers' interests in local elections.
- The **Neighbourhood Working Group**'s aim is to form active groups comprising residents and business owners from the city's various neighbourhoods. The groups should aspire to become sustainable alternatives that voice the neighbourhood's issues by consolidating residents' efforts.

Buongiorno Livorno

Good morning, Livorno

buongiornolivorno.it
Livorno, Italy

Buongiorno Livorno is an antiracist and antifascist political association, independent of traditional political parties, which was founded in November 2013 thanks to the activities of women and men engaged in a variety of social struggles: neighbourhood committees, environmental groups, groups fighting forced evictions, workers, part-time workers and the unemployed, students and others.

The collective dimension is fundamental to the group: 'A good day comes from a good discussion'; decisions are always taken in groups.

In 2014 it took part, along with three other local groupings, in the local elections, which took place at the same time as the European ones. The result was a surprise. They came in third, behind two parties with major national and international presence.

Through their actions, and by the texts that they published daily via a variety of social platforms, they opposed the increasing number of evictions, which often accompanied job losses and/or extremely precarious working conditions; they were opposed to the destruction of the environment (which for them is intimately connected with the sea and the coastline) and of the urban and cultural heritage of Livorno's citizens; they fought against attacks on welfare, especially healthcare and public education; they dealt with the effects of the floods that hit the city in September 2017, killing eight people and causing disasters throughout the area: houses flooded, rivers bursting their banks, raging waters, fallen trees, impassable streets.

In addition to this, Buongiorno Livorno hopes to create economic districts which, beyond the official limits of the city, will support and value the current local reality in particular places and the potential which until now has been ignored by a blind and centralist political culture; they wish to protect public heritage and common wealth, not just the natural resources of the city, but also its historic buildings and cultural areas; they aim to increase participatory democracy at an institutional level, calling for a government that is citizen-led and fully participative; they want, to cut a long story short, to support the neomunicipalist perspective they believe in and for which they work every day.

Cambiamo Messina dal Basso
Let's Change Messina from Below

cambiamomessinadalbasso.it
Messina, Italy

Cambiamo Messina dal Basso is a self-organized citizen movement in Messina, Sicily, made up of ordinary people, associations, leftwing parties and social movements. It has a rainbow logo, symbolizing the different backgrounds of its members.

The movement's main aims are the revitalization of the civic waterfront; the recognition of equal opportunities; the commons; the active participation of citizens in political life; and cultural change.

When it first stood for, and won, the local elections in June

2013, Cambiamo Messina dal Basso became the first civic-political movement to run a major city in Italy.

After its first electoral victory the movement continued to grow and evolve. Its activists worked to write a 'Charter of Intent', setting out the values, goals and structure of the movement, which all members must sign up to.

The movement holds weekly meetings to discuss political issues and take decisions. It regularly discusses issues and organizes common actions with the municipal administration, respecting the autonomy and role of the mayor, city council, municipal administration and citizen movement.

Cambiamo Messina dal Basso promotes networking between territorial associations and citizens; the movement encourages any form of participation, regardless of labels and flags.

Cambiamo Messina dal Basso governed Messina for two terms under Mayor Renato Accorinti, from 2013 to 2018.

Cidadâos Por Lisboa
Citizens for Lisbon

cidadaosporlisboa.pt
Lisbon, Portugal

Citizens for Lisbon (CPL), created in 2007, is a centre-left political movement that brings together individuals, activists, members of political groups, civic movements, and cultural and social associations around the goal of making Lisbon a city for all. CPL believes that a better, more open, cohesive, participative, inclusive, people-friendly and increasingly well-governed Lisbon is possible.

In 2007, CPL ran for the municipal elections and had two city councillors elected. Following the elections, political analysis on the possibility of a rightwing turn and the fact that municipal electoral law does not allow coalitions between parties and citizen groups, CPL decided to present a coalition agreement with the Socialist Party (PS). In 2009, the PS and the CPL movement signed the agreement, in a pioneering attitude of opening the parties to citizens' movements and vice versa. This agreement guaranteed common policies but safeguarded each organization's autonomy and identity.

The CPL movement believe that cities will only be able to resist and assert themselves if citizens and public opinion are mobilized and organized in national, European and global networks of cities. Bearing this in mind, the CPL defines its action around five priorities: housing, health, social rights, education and mobility, always with participation, accountability and transparency as its political orientation. It also recognizes the need to defend Lisbon's uniqueness, and reinforce its social energy, while not leaving anyone behind.

We renewed the political agreement in 2013 and again in 2017, taking up government responsibilities for Social Rights (João Afonso, 2013-17), Housing and Local Development (Paula Marqués, 2013-17 and 2017-21) and Finance Sector, Human Resources and Information Systems (João Paulo Saraiva, 2013-17 and 2017-21).

Ciudad Futura
Future City

ciudadfutura.com.ar
Rosario, Argentina

Ciudad Futura is an autonomous political instrument born from the coming-together of two social movements (Giros and the 26 June Movement), both of which have been fighting, for more than 10 years, to transform an unjust and unequal reality. Thus two structural battles in the city met each other and started to *exist* together: the struggle against property speculation, aimed at gaining access to the land; and the struggle against drug trafficking and urban violence, aimed at gaining access to justice.

This was the background against which the backbone of Ciudad Futura was created: it is a movement predicated on *prefiguring*. Ciudad Futura considers ways of constructing autonomous territorial spaces that contain within themselves the invention, sustainability and tools for development that anticipate *today* the egalitarian city that will be built tomorrow. Moving far beyond the logic of electoral competition, these forms of social management (two secondary schools, a kindergarten, a cultural centre, a farm producing milk and dairy products, and a collaborative consumer network, among other things) make real the idea of a politics radically tied to a full-scale transformation of what a city can be.

This is how Ciudad Futura is put together, following a logic of *movement*, which allows us not simply to present a different discourse from that of traditional politics, but also to show a different *way* of doing things, one that is visible, expansive and scalable. Our objective is to feminize politics, to collectively build a new type of power, the power of the common person. This was how in 2012 both organizations decided to build a political instrument that would allow them to bring into state institutions the territorial struggles they were in the process of developing. Ciudad Futura, as the political party of the movement, stood in the municipal legislative elections of 2015 and won 16 per cent of the votes, which allowed it to position itself as the third force in the city.

Coalizione Civica per Bologna
Civic Coalition for Bologna

coalizionecivica.it
Bologna, Italy

Coalizione Civica is a municipalist platform born in Bologna in the summer of 2015 with the goal of running for the June 2016 administrative elections. It was created by activists with the common goal of offering a new, alternative Left with the ambition of governing Bologna.

Focusing on a bottom-up approach, Coalizione Civica's electoral programme for Bologna was drawn up through citizen participation. Not only did Coalizione Civica run open primaries in order to establish its candidate for mayor; the lists for city and borough councillor candidates were also open to the public and subject to vote. The organization received an overall vote of just over 7 per cent (reaching 14 per cent in some boroughs) in the 2016 elections, electing two city councillors and four borough councillors who are currently in office and sit on the opposition of the Democratic Party.

Its politics are based on unifying and representing the 99 per cent, without distinctions of any kind. Its key battles are public education, common spaces, freedom of movement and the right to the city, acceptance and inclusion, sustainable transport and the environment, welfare, right to housing, municipalist practices and labour rights.

All its bodies are gender-balanced, with dual presidencies: there is a male and a female president of the association and a male and a female president of the assembly of members.

Coalizione Civica per Padova
Civic Coalition for Padua

coalizionecivicapadova.it
Padua, Italy

Over the past few years, Padua has seen its various reputations – as a city of culture, and as a place of solidarity, of voluntary service, of positivity – ruined by an administration which is closed to dialogue and dedicated to obscurantism and reducing the quality of life of its citizens. Coalizione Civica is an open and autonomous project that aims to engage citizens, as well as civic, social, economic and local political forces, with the aim of constructing a new and alternative political project. A project of rebirth, based on the fundamental points set out in the Call to Action of October 2016 – a document that has been signed to date by more than 2,000 citizens – which calls for cultural, economic and social development while protecting the environment, the individual, and the ideals of transparency and citizen participation.

The plenary assembly is the sovereign body of Coalizione Civica: it is made up of all the citizens who have decided to participate in this project of change for the city.

From the start, everyone has been able to assume responsibility for proposing, building and affirming proposals for the city council, in order to build an alternative plan that could change citizens' lives. The true wealth of Coalizione Civica is to be found in its working groups, which are made up of people who put their knowledge freely at the service of the common good. The fruit of this work is the coalition's programme. And this has led to the current situation, in which Coalizione Civica attempts to implement the programme in the new majority ruling group of the city, where it is the largest party.

The group's aim is to increase the level of participation as much as possible in the city, which will consolidate Coalizione Civica as it develops into a political workshop for the active populace, transforming government institutions from below. We need to increase our actions on the peripheries of the city and in the suburbs, which is where the strongest urban contradictions are to be found.

Compostela Aberta
Open Compostela

compostelaaberta.org
Santiago de Compostela, Spain

Compostela Aberta is a collective proposal of the citizens of Santiago de Compostela and a political-social convergence of conscientious and committed individuals. It came into being with the aim of giving the city back to its people and ending the corrupt practices that came to characterize the government of the Partido Popular, which had two mayors forced out of their seats after legal challenges, and managed to install a third mayor who had not been properly elected.

Compostela Aberta is a space born of a desire for unity, where social activists and people with political experience can work together. The coming-together of the social Left and the political Left made Compostela Aberta into a communal project which put people at the centre of public policy.

Participation and transparency are the two key axes along which the group plans any action.

The group takes all its decisions in assembly and with the support of its specialized working groups, which are essential to the construction of Compostela Aberta's political programme. The working groups are open to anyone who desires to participate in them, and they allow debate, discussion and participation to take place, and for ideas to be brought up from all areas of public discourse.

Compostela Aberta is a markedly feminist grouping, with equal institutional representation; it strongly supports actions by the government and by itself as an organization to promote policies of equality as a transversal tool in its work. It is also an organization that is markedly ecosocial in its make-up, focused not only on the conservation of the environment but also on the efficient management of public resources and an insistence on policies aimed towards benefiting society as a whole.

Comú de Lleida
Commons of Lleida

comudelleida.cat
Lleida, Spain

Comú de Lleida is a grouping of individuals from the city of Lleida who have organized themselves in order to participate in municipal politics by winning electoral representation, under the basic principles of promoting the common good, encouraging participation in the democratic process, and transparency.

It was founded in 2013 as a citizens' initiative in order to create a convergence candidacy that would unite individuals from various political parties as well as citizens who were politically active, and that would help change the way the city was governed. The only political party whose support it received was the Piratas de Cataluña party, so it opted instead to put up a citizen candidacy in the form of a group of voters, which won 3,787 votes and two council posts in the 2015 elections.

Comú de Lleida aims to increase citizen participation in municipal politics by moving beyond ideological labels and bringing to the forefront shared objectives that will result in better organization and management of common goods, in order to help Lleida's citizens as much as possible.

Comú de Lleida is committed to a brand of politics in the service of the people and run by the people. Some of the main principles by which Comú de Lleida runs and organizes itself are as follows: citizen participation, transparency, 'traceability' (following the lines of supply and production throughout all aspects of the city government), the promotion of socially oriented and generally useful economic policies, an insistence on presenting a viable and fair budget to the city, an insistence on basic rights for citizens, the elimination of political privileges, and formulating a model for the city that is built around its citizens and respect for the environment.

Comú de Lleida is organized via an assembly and various working groups that are open to all who share the basic ideals of the project, support its organizational framework and endorse its code of ethics. Decisions are taken by consensus, or, in exceptional cases, by mechanisms which allow for decisions by a significant majority. Elected representatives are subject to a code of ethics that includes limitation of their mandates, limitation of their salaries, an obligation to transparency and a declaration of conflicts of interest.

Cooperation Jackson

cooperationjackson.org
Jackson, Mississippi, US

Cooperation Jackson is an emerging vehicle for sustainable community development, economic democracy and community ownership in Jackson, Mississippi. Founded in 2014, its basic theory of change is centred on the position that organizing and empowering the structurally under- and unemployed sectors of the working class, particularly from

Black and Latino communities, to build worker-organized and owned co-operatives will be a catalyst for the democratization of the economy and society overall.

Its broad mission is to advance the development of economic democracy by building a solidarity economy anchored by a network of co-operatives and other types of worker-owned and democratically self-managed enterprises. To do this it organizes to promote universal access to common resources, democratize the ownership of the means of production, and democratize all the essential processes of production and distribution through worker self-management and sustainable consumption.

It is implementing its vision through four interconnected and interdependent institutions: an emerging federation of local worker co-operatives, a developing co-operative incubator, a co-operative education and training centre, and a co-operative bank or financial institution.

Building upon a century-old tradition from the National Negro Convention Movement, Cooperation Jackson has participated in the use of open 'people's assemblies' to give voice to local concerns, train new leaders, build coalitions and engage more effectively in public policy. Through these assemblies, Jackson began to gain institutional power, which resulted in the successful election of Chokwe Lumumba to mayor in 2013, and again with the election of his son, Chokwe Antar Lumumba, in 2017.

These major victories in the electoral realm have the potential to create space for solidarity economy mechanisms to be more popularized and expanded upon in Jackson, pushing Jackson to be a sustainable city transitioning from an extractive economy to one that empowers working people and is ecologically aligned with the planet.

Cooperation Jackson is the realization of a Just Transition vision decades in the making. Its roots lie deep within the struggle for democratic rights, economic justice and self-determination, particularly for people of African descent in the Deep South, and dignity for all workers.

Fearless Cities

Crida per Sabadell
Call for Sabadell

cridapersabadell.cat
Sabadell, Spain

Crida per Sabadell is a political organization that aims to encourage citizens to organize themselves to take the reins in city neighbourhoods and put institutions at the service of the public. In order to do this, our everyday work is based half in the streets and half in the institutions themselves.

In the streets, we set up political campaigns, self-governing groups and local working groups.

The self-governing groups are thematic groups that work on concrete proposals they aim to apply, either from the streets or from governmental organizations, to all aspects of communal life: energy, housing, food, family care, productivity, public spaces, culture, education and so on.

The local working groups work in conjunction with the community in each area of the city in order to pass on ideas, deal with problems and create networks of mutual support and organization throughout the city.

Crida per Sabadell is currently represented in the city's local government. It participates in the bodies that deal with public services, housing, citizen participation and civil rights. Its aim is to apply a programme of social transformation throughout Sabadell.

This programme contains the following elements:

- **Citizen's audit of the council.** The aim is to shed light on political and economic corruption: all cases of corruption from former administrations are to be brought to court and irregularities are to be brought to light, especially in cases of people in positions of authority who used their posts for their own benefit and against the general good of the populace.
- **Put a halt to the situation of social emergency.** Crida per Sabadell aims to offer proposals for viable alternatives to this and, if necessary, disobey the laws that are perpetuated by the unjust economic system. Citizens' rights and

170

social wellbeing are to be put at the centre of political debate.

- **Democratize local government**. Institutions are there to serve the people. They are to be used as a tool that serves the public and which operates with complete transparency. Local government should be a tool for social intervention, which promotes citizen participation in all political decisions.

CUP de Celrà – Poble Actiu
CUP of Celrà – Active People

celra.cup.cat
Celrà, Spain

The CUP is an assembly-based political organization that is present in all areas that make up the territory of the *Països Catalans*, and which works together to create a country that is independent, socialist, ecologically sustainable, territorially balanced and freed from all forms of patriarchal domination.

The CUP presents itself as a space which is available to all people and groups that aim to transform Catalonia and who work for the freedom of our people: it aims to be a zone of confluence for popular movements that fight for the national and social liberation of the *Països Catalans*.

The CUP is an avowedly socialist organization, which aims to substitute the capitalist socio-economic model for a new one that is focused on collective human needs and a respect for the environment. It works along the following axes: it defends the political rights of the Catalan people; it defends the political rights of the working classes; it defends equality; it defends the land against ecological and urbanizing assaults; it promotes feminism and sexual and gender liberation; and it defends national languages and identities, and internationalism, as a way of promoting egalitarian, anti-colonial and fraternal relations among peoples.

Via its local assemblies, the CUP carries out its political activities both inside and outside the institutions of local government. Although it understands the limited scope for action from within local government, the CUP is working to transform regionalist municipalism in order to put forward a new vision of Catalonia based on the municipality as a space that is closer and more attentive to the individual and his or her needs.

The Celrà CUP is organized into different thematic working groups, where local assembly activists meet and which regularly organize open municipal meetings. The main current areas of activity are waste disposal, working with groups that support young socio-economically disadvantaged individuals in order to get them back into work or education, the consolidation and expansion of the Municipal Office of Support for the Elderly, and managing the city's land in an environmentally sustainable way, via social or co-operative initiatives that aim to support local assets and generate decently waged and dignified jobs.

Decide Roma
Rome Decides

decideroma.com
Rome, Italy

Decide Roma came into being following the public demonstration under the banner 'Rome is not for sale', which was organized at the beginning of 2016 and aimed to block property speculation in the city, as well as to strengthen the self-managed areas of the city, to call for an open audit of the local government's public debt and return democratic choice to the hands of the citizens of Rome.

Decide Roma is a collective project that aims to take control of politics from the ground up: the power to take decisions, which has been so long sequestered within a particularly narrow political framework, needs to be returned to the people. Over time, citizens' faith in their representatives has faded away, and now it is only direct participation and overt struggles that can lead to meaningful change. Citizen participation is not something that can be made manifest in a few votes at irregular elections.

For us, one of the main objects of our interest is the question of public property, of its use and management. More than simply the question of public spaces, this idea also includes public use of public services, which is currently being put into jeopardy as work becomes ever more precarious and previously public utilities and spaces are privatized.

Our proposed programme is set out in the *Carta di Roma Comune* (Charter of Our Common Rome), which has been thrashed out and developed over hundreds of public meetings. The *Carta* sets out the foundational principles of a new way by which all citizens can be included and given a role within the 'public system'. It can be summed up in three key words: common urban goods.

The only way to change the system is to encourage citizen participation and decentralize power. Corruption is always created when a government of the many is replaced by one of the few. A brave and forward-facing set of policies is one that acknowledges that the populace, beyond the formal moment of public elections, has the right to decide its own fate: not simply to decide who governs them, but to decide how they will be governed.

Demokratik Toplum Kongresi
Democratic Society Congress

kcd-dtk.org
Turkish Kurdistan

The Democratic Society Congress (DTK), set up in Bakur in 2007, is an independent, non-governmental umbrella structure that aims to establish democratic confederalism in Bakur (the area of Kurdistan within the borders of Turkey). Democratic confederalism describes stateless confederations of self-governing, grassroots assemblies, working according to anti-capitalist, feminist and ecological principles.

The Congress stands against religious, national, ethnic,

cultural and gender inequality and injustice, and against war and militarism. It defends the rights and freedoms of all peoples of Turkey and Kurdistan, including the right to democratic autonomy. According to the DTK, democratic autonomy is not about changing the borders of nation-states; rather it is about strengthening the ties of fraternity and promoting unity in diversity within existing borders. Democratic autonomy is not a state-building or a state-abolishing project; it's a process of a continual development and construction that seeks less state and more society.

The DTK operates as a parliament with the aim of creating a new society under the weight of repression of the existing one. It upholds that a wide range of societal problems can only be overcome through freedom of thought and the right to organize. It is made up of 501 delegates, who meet every three months. Of these, 301 are directly elected to represent local assemblies of people living in the region, while 200 places are reserved for representatives of political parties, civil-society organizations, municipalities and non-Kurdish delegates.

A minimum of 50 per cent of all DTK delegates must be women, and all presidential and leadership roles are held jointly by a man and a woman. The DTK's two co-chairs and 21-member executive council are elected by its 501 delegates for two-year terms.

The DTK has 14 different commissions, covering issues such as ecology, economy, education, language, public affairs, religion, culture, science, diplomacy, women and young people.

Demosistō
Standing-Up People

demosisto.hk
Hong Kong

Demosistō aims to achieve democratic self-determination in Hong Kong. Through direct action, popular referenda and nonviolent means, the party pushes for the city's political and economic autonomy from the oppression of the Communist Party of China (CPC) and capitalist hegemony.

Demosistō is a movement-based party. It is developing a new civic engagement platform for political discussion among citizens, in order to encourage grassroots social movements and to strengthen interaction across all sectors of civil society. It trusts the community to realize the common good and to build a city of multiplicity, equality and justice.

Since the 1997 handover to China, Hong Kong has been under the authoritarian rule of the CPC and capitalist hegemony. Hong Kongers have demonstrated steadfast resistance to their exploitative socio-economic system through the anti-Article 23 rally of 2003 and the anti-High Speed Rail movement of 2010. These protests have moulded society by creating a path for future mass movements in Hong Kong.

During the 2012 anti-National Education Campaign, students rose up and successfully forced the government to abolish a curriculum that whitewashed communist history. Two years later, the Umbrella Movement arose in response to the CPC's broken promise of political reform. This movement redefined Hong Kong, and brought the city into a new era: an era of resistance.

Demosistō was founded to lead this journey: to unite citizens with the goal of obtaining autonomy for their Hong Kong.

Guanyem Badalona en Comú
Let's Win Badalona Together

guanyembadalona.org
Badalona, Spain

Guanyem Badalona en Comú is a municipalist platform that came into being in February 2015 out of a convergence of individuals who came from several political movements and municipalist groupings in order to transform municipal politics, which was at that time controlled by the extreme Right. The aim was to put local government at the service of the needs of all the city's inhabitants. In the municipal elections of 2015 Guanyem Badalona managed to become the second-placed grouping and it ran the local government in coalition with other political groups, with Dolors Sabater as mayor, until June 2018.

Guanyem Badalona en Comú is an assembly-based group, organized into district groups and programme groups, with a co-ordinator and a debating council. In its local seat, in the La Salut district, it has set into motion the Ateneu Carme Claramunt, a political movement aimed at increasing popular unity.

Its programme, which is open to outside participation and developed in a participative fashion, is founded on three pillars: a democratic revolution, social justice, and the establishment, street by street, of a Catalan republic.

The people who work for Guanyem Badalona En Comú are permitted to earn a maximum of three and a half times the minimum wage. Most of the money left over from their salary provision is put into a fund for social projects, the 'Pot Comú', which gathered 30,000 euros over 2015-16.

While in control of the municipal government, Guanyem Badalona reversed the programme of cuts to public spending and emphasized policies aimed at improving social and cultural conditions, increasing coexistence between communities, and promoting social housing and rent support. It also developed citizen participation in significant ways, such as by inaugurating a participative process to decide where 50 per cent of the sums available for investment were to be allocated.

On 20 June 2018, Guanyem Badalona En Comú was removed from office through a motion of no confidence passed thanks to an alliance between the Catalan Socialist Party (PSC) and the Popular Party.

Halklarin Demokratik Partisi
Peoples' Democratic Party

hdp.org.tr
Turkey

The Peoples' Democratic Party (HDP) was founded in the summer of 2013, shortly after the Gezi protests engulfed Turkey. Rooted in the pro-Kurdish political movement, the new party aimed to unite leftist and marginalized groups across the country. The HDP's appeal was demonstrated when it won 80 seats in the 550-seat parliament in the June 2015 Turkish national elections.

The HDP advocates a strongly decentralized Turkey, with municipalist and autonomous bottom-up structures to replace the currently highly centralized government. It has put forward the idea of 'democratic autonomy', a political framework based upon communal democracy, where power is exercised at the local level. Democratic autonomy is about redesigning public space so that citizens can assemble at the municipal level to discuss daily issues of an economic, political, cultural and social nature. It is believed that the road to an egalitarian society can only emerge from inclusive political structures in which people of all classes participate in decision-making processes.

The HDP is well known for being a pluralist, inclusive and feminist platform. The party addresses critical questions such as Kurdish rights, the environment, workers' rights, religious rights, LGBT rights and women's empowerment. The party's electoral candidates have included members of different ethnic and religious backgrounds, as well as sexual minorities and a high proportion of women. Above all, women's rights occupy a special place within the party agenda, with various gender parity measures in place to support this through representation (co-leadership, electoral lists, parliament, and so on).

The HDP's current concerns are to improve basic freedoms in Turkey, stop the ongoing war between Kurdish rebels and Turkish forces, disengage from capitalist projects, continue

177

libertarian municipalist politics, drastically reduce domestic violence, and address the ecological crisis facing our Earth.

Independents for Frome

iffrome.org.uk
Frome, UK

Independents for Frome (ifF) was created in 2011 by a group of people who felt the potential of local government was not being met. In particular they were clear that national political dogma and ideology were not relevant at a local level – yet these were what drove the current local agenda for a market town with a population of 26,000 people in rural England.

Some quick research revealed that groups of truly independents rarely – if ever – got elected. Most non-party candidates either have extreme views, or focus on a single issue. IfF therefore developed 'Ways of Working' which defined core values and a methodology of co-operation. When it ran for office, ifF offered no manifesto, just a description of how it would operate in a more participative way if elected.

In the 2011 local election, turnout rose by 75 per cent and ifF won 10 out of the 17 seats on the town council. It quickly rewrote the rule book, re-engineering the ways the council operated (creating a style of council meetings that allowed for local people to have their say and join in debates) and elevating the agenda and vision for the council.

In 2017 ifF won all 17 seats, despite opposition from all political parties in every area.

The council has continued to experiment with ways of working – within the councillor group, with staff and with the public. This has resulted in a breadth of interests centred around sustainability, wellbeing and prosperity.

Independents for Frome has created a lot of interest in its achievements and ways of working and has inspired similar movements in other small towns in England, including Buckfastleigh, Bradford-on-Avon, Monmouth and Alderley Edge.

Koalicja TAK!
YES! Coalition

takdlalodzi.pl
Łódź, Poland

Koalicja TAK! is a municipalist group from the city of Łódź, which was set up in 2017 in order to participate in the 2018 local elections. It is made up of different political groupings centred on civil rights, women's rights and national issues, such as Łódzkie Dziewuchy Dziewuchom (Gals 4 Gals), Krytyka Polityczna (Political Criticism) and Inicjatywa Polska (Polish Initiative), as well as numerous local activists.

Its aims as a movement are to improve the quality of daily life, and to introduce programmes that will help people to escape poverty and neglect, and improve their living conditions. Łódź is currently a city of clear contrasts when it comes to the economic situation, living standards and opportunities for education. One of its great problems is that of gentrification.

Koalicja TAK! aims to change the city's priorities when it comes to urban investment. The current focus of local government in Łódź is large-scale investment, such as support for sports stadia and international exhibitions (for example Expo 2022, which will take place in Łódź). The authorities are focusing the development of the city's transport infrastructure on private vehicles, ignoring public transport and the needs of pedestrians. Advances that had been made in public participation in the democratic process have slowed as well.

Koalicja TAK! is currently running open workshops with citizens from all over Łódź, in order to establish a coherent political programme for the city. We have just become a civic association and in March 2018 we opened a social centre, a communal area where courses can be taught and where people are free to come and share their problems and their ideas for solutions.

Our chief values are those of equality and dignity – dignity for minorities, for women, and for people in precarious socio-economic positions – and encouraging a decent standard of living for the many, not the few. We wish to develop Łódź into a city that is environmentally friendly and welcoming.

Lepszy Gdańsk
A Better Gdańsk

Gdańsk, Poland

The old and proud city of Gdańsk has been in need of a viable alternative for years and the creation of Lepszy Gdańsk is the answer: a progressive grassroots movement set up by the people and for the people. We are the alternative to the old politics, to vested interests and anachronistic neoliberal policies whose primary goal is to reverse local priorities in line with the constitutional and statutory principles of the social market economy.

Small, regional investments that serve communities are more important than large, symbolic projects. Education should not fall prey to austerity policy, but instead become one of the priorities of our local government. Social policy, understood as a package of communal services available to the widest possible group of residents, should be an ordinary element of our everyday life. Participation, understood as a dialogue between different groups of residents and their representatives, is a necessity. Democracy must not just be a comfortable slogan on paper. Lepszy Gdańsk wants a real revolution in decision-making, transparency of action, economical and balanced management of communal resources, officials who treat their jobs as a service to society. We oppose the unlimited privatization of communal property and the deterioration of urban space through its unrestricted commercialization and subordination to developer interests. We want real change at the political, social and grassroots levels. We want a better city.

The eight theses of Lepszy Gdańsk:

1 Let us revive local entrepreneurship.
2 We will promote district investment projects.
3 We must make science and culture a driving force for the city's development.

4 Let us change the city's transport policy.

5 Let residents decide about their city.

6 We must adjust our social policy to the needs of residents.

7 Education is not a place for savings.

8 Let us limit the privatization of municipal resources and services in Gdańsk.

Lepszy Gdańsk is a founding member of the Congress of Urban Movements.

Málaga Ahora
Malaga Now

malagaahora.org/
Málaga, Spain

Málaga Ahora is not a political party (although when we put up candidates at the 2015 municipal election it was under this name). Neither is it a grouping of indistinct acronyms or a pact between organizations. Málaga Ahora is a citizens' initiative that aims at the convergence of a number of common democratic practices and aims, bringing together individuals as well as the different social, neighbourhood, cultural and political groups of the city. This is a challenge that requires new spaces for organization and social participation, in order to encourage political participation in new, non-traditional ways, to make institutional actions reflect the true demands of the populace.

The institutional activity of Málaga Ahora is only one of its areas of action, as the group also supports the work of neighbourhood groups, social and citizen movements that have for decades been calling for a city that is respectable, inhabitable, more equal and more sustainable. The policy of confluence, and the search for common ground, acknowledges the richness and the diversity that come from having a variety of points of view, and calls for general co-operation in areas that concern the common good.

The 2015 elections turned Málaga Ahora into the third-largest political force in Malaga local government, and won them four councillors (as well as a provincial deputy, although the movement only stood in the capital). Three of these councillors were women: the policy of having 'zip lists' (lists of candidates where men and women are represented and in theory elected in equal numbers) was only used in the case of female under-representation, and the primary elections for candidates had given Málaga Ahora two women in the top two spots.

Currently, Málaga Ahora is the only group in the history of local government in Malaga to be made up of only women, as the male councillor left his position in October 2016 in order to work as an independent, in part because of his disagreement with the policies of horizontality and convergence embodied and enacted by the group.

Marea Atlántica
Atlantic Tide

mareatlantica.org
A Coruña, Spain

Marea Atlántica is a municipalist platform made up of participating citizens, which was set up in A Coruña, a medium-sized coastal town of 250,000 inhabitants. It is a political space that exists to encourage the convergence of traditional political parties with activist groups and previously unaffiliated individuals, who agree to work together to regain control of local institutions and bring them back under the control of the community. The 'mareantes', the people who work with and take part in the Marea Atlántica, always do so as individuals, regardless of any other political affiliations they might have.

Using a rough manifesto as a point of departure, the group created a participative process, generous and without any particular focal individuals, which ran a municipalist candidacy at the local elections of May 2015. It managed to go from nowhere to being the most-voted-for party and ended up in a technical draw with the conservative Partido Popular, with 31 per cent of the vote. This allowed it, after some wrangling, to form by itself the new municipal government in A Coruña.

Its arrival into local government did not prevent the organization from maintaining an activist presence, alongside its work in government, in some of the most important social battles in the city, such as defending the city's inner harbour against property speculators. This work has not been free of political and organizational complications, which should not be overlooked.

Marea Atlántica, since the first days of its existence, has developed its own working methodology based on trust, mutual aid and consensus, with the aim of avoiding the delays and confusions that are typical of partisan politics. Its feminist focus is also an important part of the organization, from an insistence on absolute equality in representation to the promotion of female participation in assembly meetings. We also work according to a code of ethics that controls the behaviour of the governing group and which is based on a few clear basic principles, such as radical democracy, concern for the environment, respect for diversity and the struggle for social justice.

Massa Critica
Critical Mass

massacriticanapoli.org
Naples, Italy

Massa Critica is a citizen platform independent of the city government. It came into being in the autumn of 2015 and aimed to make a political intervention in the electoral debates of the following spring in Naples and to build a large space for public debate, making the public's desire for discussion about, participation in and appraisal of their local government its key concern.

The aim of Massa Critica is to establish itself within local government in order to carry on with its strategy of active resistance; it is this strategy that makes Naples a key testing-ground for self-government and local organization, and which has led it in certain instances to set the agenda for the way in which municipal government is carried out in Italy.

The key idea on which the activities of Massa Critica are based is that, in the current phase of historical development, we need to take back control of the argument about the future of the city, and begin a process which aims to break through the barriers that have held social movements back over the years. We have to make serious and pertinent decisions about how development is to take place, what our relationship with the environment is to be, and how we are to manage work and poor employment prospects: all notions which have been up till now abandoned or ignored by people with control at the institutional level.

Massa Critica is currently developing via working groups that focus on the following: democracy and self-determination; work, public services and public finance; the environment, land use in the city and rights of access to it; culture, education and research.

To bring so many people together is not the same as turning them into a uniform mass, as might happen with a traditional political party, but rather it means creating spaces for debate that make dialogue possible and promote different points of view and collective planning. This is the common spirit that we have been fostering since the autumn of 2015, and which has only spread further and developed over time, putting new topics onto its cultural and political agenda: the transformation of how the platform is organized; the redefinition of the platform's plan of political intervention within the government from outside, its 'assault' on the structures of power; and the construction of a political space made up of a network of cities at the European and international level.

Miasto jest Nasze
The City is Ours

miastojestnasze.org
Warsaw, Poland

Miasto jest Nasze is a Warsaw-based non-profit civic association, founded in 2013 by a group of social activists, which has become a major urban movement in Poland. It has always relied on the voluntary work of its members, who are passionate about improving the city and quality of life of its inhabitants. Currently, it brings together more than a hundred members from all walks of life, with the oldest being born before the Second World War, and the youngest still in secondary school.

Since its beginnings, Miasto jest Nasze has been active in identifying and addressing a number of issues in Warsaw, such as chaotic urban planning and lack of architectural policies (such as problems related to land ownership or uncontrolled advertising), as well as deficiencies in the transport network and infrastructure. The association publicizes controversial decisions made by the local authorities, brings to light examples of nepotism in city management, and ensures that citizens' voices are heard in the decision-making process. It supports transparency across all city functions as well as civic participation through participatory budgets and public consultations.

Miasto jest Nasze champions a more resident-friendly and greener city, highlighting the need for sustainable development. It serves as an active watchdog, verifying that all city investments follow environmental principles and regulations. For example, it was one of the first organizations to point out the problem of heavy air pollution in Warsaw and its harmful effects on human health. The mission of Miasto jest Nasze is to build on positive initiatives that bring communities together. For that reason, the organization decided to take part in the local government elections in November 2014, succeeding in three districts in Warsaw.

Miasto Wspólne
Common City

miastowspolne.org
Kraków, Poland

Miasto Wspólne is a non-profit association and urban movement in Kraków, Poland. It promotes citizens' right to the city, social participation in decision-making and transparency in local government. The association focuses on socio-spatial justice and the democratization of municipal politics. It campaigns to influence the local political process through a range of activities, from grassroots mobilization, protests and media appearances to watchdog actions aimed at monitoring the activity of the city council and municipality. Miasto Wspólne co-operates with other citizens' organizations in advancing social justice and equality, sustainable growth, accessible public services, environmental protection and cultural diversity. Members of Miasto Wspólne come from diverse backgrounds, including grassroots activism, NGOs and academia.

The association originates from the movement Kraków Przeciw Igrzyskom (Kraków Against the Games), which successfully campaigned against holding the Winter Olympics in Kraków. The initiative gathered considerable public support and the Olympic project was rejected in a referendum by almost 70 per cent of voters. In 2014 Kraków Przeciw Igrzyskom stood in the local elections, but despite considerable support (7 per cent) was not able to secure seats on the city council.

Currently Miasto Wspólne is involved in two projects focused on housing, transparency and corruption. It provides legal assistance for persons threatened by eviction and co-ordinates a watchdog project 'Social Audit of Restitution', aimed at fighting unjust and illegal reprivatization of housing in Kraków. Miasto Wspólne gathered a broad coalition for the local elections in 2018.

Movimiento Valparaíso Ciudadano
Valparaíso Citizens' Movement

Valparaíso, Chile

Movimiento Valparaíso Ciudadano aims to build an empowered, conscious citizenry with the capacity for individual and collective action in the city of Valparaíso. It sees the citizen mayoralty of Jorge Sharpe and its citizen councillors as instruments to support its transformative goals.

At the same time, Movimiento Valparaíso Ciudadano is independent of the city government, with its own agenda, which promotes the binding participation of citizens in making decisions that affect them.

The citizen mayoralty was driven by a set of local political organizations and movements, including Movimiento Valparaíso Ciudadano. Its programme is centred on improving the life of residents by conserving the city's coast and relationship with the sea; defending individual and collective rights, within a value framework that gives dignity to its citizens; taking care of the environment; and promoting relations of solidarity, collaboration, mutual respect and equity.

The citizen mayoralty began with the primaries for the municipal elections in mid-2016 and was consolidated with the victory of Jorge Sharpe in October of the same year. Since taking office in December 2016, the administration has driven a local development strategy while promoting transformative participation of the territory.

Muitas pela Cidade que Queremos
Many for the City We Want

somosmuitas.com.br
Belo Horizonte, Brazil

Muitas pela Cidade que Queremos is a municipalist citizens' movement that came into being in Belo Horizonte in 2015. It is inspired by other municipalist movements around the world, as well as by specifically Latin American experiences and traditional Brazilian methods of community organization. Its stated aim was to 'occupy the elections bravely, using citizen power' and, in order to do this, individuals, both independent activists and members of various movements, collectives and parties, united around a framework that was horizontal and collaborative. Its chief principles were as follows: policies that were feminist and anti-racist; encouraging as wide a confluence as possible of progressive forces; promoting diversity, representativeness, transparency, a search for the common good, and the radicalization of democracy.

In the 2016 municipal elections, Muitas ran 12 candidates, representing, among other groups and interests, women, black people, indigenous people, young people, LGBTIQ people, the struggle for access to the city and culture, and environmental protection. In order to deconstruct the focus that politics generally has on individuals, the collective campaign had as its slogan 'A vote for one is a vote for all'. In an election that was notable for its rejection of old-fashioned political tropes, Muitas recruited a number of volunteers, who helped it to win over the streets and maintain a vital internet presence, which promoted and amplified the inchoate desire that was present throughout the city for a new kind of city with a new type of politics. Áurea Carolina and Cida Falabella both won places on Belo Horizonte's municipal council, with Áurea receiving the most votes of any councillor in the history of the city.

This was how the Gabinetona, the political grouping headed by Áurea Carolina and Cida Falabella (along with their unique team, which worked together in an open-plan space), came into being. This grouping, identifying itself as open, collective and popular, made it possible for new forms of political activity within pre-existing institutional structures to be attempted, and also to offer the city direct channels for participation and social mobilization, as well as popular education, political training and communication.

Ndifuna Ukwazi
Dare to Know

nu.org.za
Cape Town, South Africa

Ndifuna Ukwazi is a non-profit activist organization and law centre that combines research, political organizing and litigation in campaigns to advance urban land justice in Cape Town. Its primary mission is to expand and protect access to affordable housing and build an integrated and inclusive city.

It works to disrupt the reproduction of spatial apartheid and inequality by compelling government to meet its obligations to use well-located land to provide affordable housing, securing inclusionary housing from the private sector, while simultaneously defending the rights and security of tenure of poor and working-class people who live in rental housing and are being forced out of the city because of rising rents, gentrification and unfair rental practices.

Ndifuna Ukwazi is a supporter of 'Reclaim the City', a Cape-Town-based movement of tenants campaigning for land and housing, providing legal support and advice, and occupying public buildings in pursuit of justice and equality.

Ne da(vi)mo Beograd
Don't let Belgrade D(r)own

nedavimobeograd.wordpress.com
Belgrade, Serbia

Ne da(vi)mo Beograd acts in the fields of urban and cultural policy, sustainable city development, fair use of common resources, and the involvement of citizens in the urban development of their environment. In 2014 the initiative united around a common goal: putting an end to the degradation and plunder of Belgrade by megalomaniacal urban and architectural projects, primarily the 'Belgrade Waterfront' project, through self-organized street actions, judicial and media activism, public campaigns and protests.

What started as an act of civil disobedience, with 100 participants objecting to the dubious Belgrade Masterplan changes, was followed by numerous guerrilla actions, public talks, research and information dissemination, media engagement, newspaper publishing, and a series of protests of more than 20,000 people on the streets, raising awareness and changing public opinion and engagement in Belgrade's urban development along the way.

At the moment, Ne da(vi)mo Beograd is working on widening dialogue at the level of local communities and neighbourhoods, in order to define citizens' problems, needs and desires and jointly elaborate common policies, whose outcome must be a better life for everyone and not for just a privileged minority. To put this into practice, the Initiative has decided to participate in the local elections for the Assembly of the City of Belgrade, and its future development will incorporate this new, democratic aspect of political struggle.

Partiya Yekîtiya Demokrat
Democratic Union Party

pydrojava.net/english
Rojava, Syrian Kurdistan

Rojava, the Kurdish-majority zone in northern Syria, is the location of a unique experiment in grassroots, participatory democracy. A landmass slightly larger than Belgium, in the midst of war, it is undergoing a profound social revolution that emphasizes social and economic equality, religious tolerance, ethnic inclusion, collectivity combined with individual freedom, ecology, and a radical feminism.

The political system of Rojava is based on a paradigm called Democratic Confederalism, articulated by imprisoned Kurdish leader Abdullah Öcalan. It is a system that does not call for a separate Kurdish state but seeks to employ self-rule to address the decades of state-sponsored genocide inflicted on the Kurds.

In Rojava, 40-50 per cent of the members of any civil society or governing body must be female, with a woman serving as co-chair in every executive or legislative office. Every member of the community can participate in decision-making as part their local 'commune', of 30 to 400 households. The board of each commune sends representatives to the Village Council, a body made up of 7 to 30 communes. In turn, the Village Council sends elected representatives to the District People's Council, which then sends delegates to the fourth level, the People's Council of West Kurdistan (MGRK). The MGRK elects members to the Movement for a Democratic Society, or TEV-DEM, which co-ordinates decisions among all three cantons of Rojava. At each of the four levels there are citizen commissions on women, defence, economics, politics, civil society, justice, ideology and free society.

Every level of the council system has a separate women's council, formed by the Kongreya Star, which organizes training sessions on women's empowerment, and whose decisions take priority over all issues affecting women. As a result, feminist and anti-capitalist ideas, and the notion of an ecological life, are flourishing across the entire society, with theories developed through a new paradigm called Jineology – the woman's science.

Portland Assembly

portlandassembly.com
Portland, Oregon, US

Portland Assembly works towards social transformation through the creation of neighbourhood programmes, education, coalition-building and direct action. It focuses on engaging the deep and ongoing historical traumas of patriarchy, colonization, capitalism, and all systems of domination and hierarchy by building networks of mutual aid and systems of dual power that support the wellbeing of everyone and provide access and voice to those who are at the least supported intersections of society.

The core of Portland Assembly's vision is the formation of Neighbourhood Action Councils (NACs): autonomous, directly democratic groups that meet regularly to work through problems together and address issues that are specific to their area. The NAC is a place to connect, share ideas, develop shared analysis through study and discussion, and to plan and take action. NACs bring project ideas to monthly Spokescouncil meetings to request resources, offer resources, or expand the project to other NACs. Neighbourhood Organizing offers a practical and accessible people-powered solution.

Starting in its NACs, Portland Assembly builds relationships of solidarity with groups and individuals within its communities to provide neighbourhood-driven and targeted programmes like resource shares, community defence training, emergency warming shelters and educational events. It has developed toolkits, training sessions and process-management systems that are scalable and able to be applied throughout the network.

Portland Assembly is building better communities, be it through mutual aid, childcare, self-defence, harm reduction, education, or addressing day-to-day neighbourhood safety in the face of harassment, deportations and police violence. NACs all around the city are already hard at work organizing their communities.

Projet Montréal
Project Montreal

en.projetmontreal.org
Montreal, Canada

Projet Montréal is a municipal political party founded in 2004. A truly democratic party, Projet Montréal stands for sustainable development, human-scale urban policies, strong public services and affordability, inclusion, integrity, transparency and participatory democracy.

Having grown its roots and its popular support in every election since 2005, Projet Montréal finally won a majority on Montréal's city council in 2017. Its leader, Valérie Plante, then became the first woman mayor in the city's 375-year history.

Projet Montréal is a grassroots, bottom-up political party. In every borough, members can form local associations to discuss policies and organize mobilization, outreach and advocacy events on the issues they care about. Local associations, as well as the party's steering committee, are run by volunteers, who are elected annually by their peers.

The party enjoys a strong internal democracy. Equality between women and men, as well as the inclusion and representation of Montréalers in all their diversity, are at the core if its principles and objectives. For example, in the last election, 50 per cent of the candidates the party ran were women, and 40 per cent were from diverse, non-majority backgrounds.

Party members firmly believe that change and innovation happens first and foremost at the local level. In every neighbourhood, Projet Montréal promotes citizen participation in public affairs through consultation. The party also supports and protects the unique character of each of Montréal's neighbourhoods, by giving borough councils enough support and autonomy to pursue their own policies and priorities relating to local, proximity services. This allows local administrations to develop creative solutions to the urban issues their residents live with every day.

Rassemblement Citoyen de la Gauche et des Écologistes
Citizen Left-Green Alliance

unevillepourtous.fr
Grenoble, France

Rassemblement Citoyen is an alliance launched in Grenoble in 2013 by citizens involved in social movements. It is supported by a mix of political parties: the EELV (France's Green Party) and the Parti de Gauche (Left Party), and local social movements. Its manifesto, '120 commitments', was drawn up through citizen participation and pursues three main goals: to renew local democracy, to build a social and environmental shield and to make Grenoble a city where everyone feels it is good to live. The organization won the May 2014 city elections, forming a majority government under the leadership of mayor Eric Piolle.

It was the first time that a team composed exclusively of greens, leftwingers and citizen movements had won a city as big as Grenoble (170,000 inhabitants). The two main national parties, the Socialist Party and the Republicans, are both in the opposition. The idea of the project is to show that alternatives are possible and to experiment with social and ecological transition at the scale of a city. Somehow, since 2014, the Alpine city has become a laboratory for pioneering reforms and projects.

Some of the reforms, such as banning advertising billboards in public places, received worldwide attention, but the alliance considers that its job is to show that another public policy, which is aligned with the emergence of a new model for society that is now inevitable, is possible. This includes a lot of less well-known examples, like limiting the height of new buildings, protecting the water table, pushing for organic school lunches, reducing the speed limit to 30 kilometres per hour, creating new green spaces inside the city, not raising local taxes, and welcoming migrants.

Richmond Progressive Alliance

richmondprogressivealliance.net
Richmond, California, US

Based in Richmond, California, a city of 110,000 where minorities are in the majority, the Richmond Progressive Alliance (RPA) is a multi-issue, multi-racial, working-class-oriented organization. It runs candidates for municipal office (winning 10 out of 16 races since 2004) and organizes local campaigns for economic justice and environmental protection.

The RPA is simultaneously an electoral formation, a membership organization, a coalition of community groups, and a key co-ordinator of grassroots education and citizen mobilization around multiple issues. Unusual in the fractious and marginalized US Left, the group unites dissident Democrats, socialists, independents, and third-party voters affiliated with the California Greens or Peace and Freedom Party.

RPA candidates have distinguished themselves locally by their refusal to accept business donations, while welcoming the support of progressive unions. The Alliance relies for its funds on membership dues, door-to-door canvassing to expand its grassroots base, and, in election years, on small individual donors and modest public matching funds for its city council and mayoral candidates. RPA's work with labour and community allies has created strong synergy between activist city-hall leadership and grassroots organizing.

The RPA's organizational success has flowed from getting people to come together, adopt a common platform, and run candidates who refuse all corporate donations and who will remain accountable to the constituencies that elected them. Once elected, RPA candidates have used their position as mayor or city councillor to help mobilize the community to counter the enormous political influence of Chevron, the city's largest employer, and other special interests.

The RPA doesn't just pop up every two or four years at election time. Its 400 fee-paying members are involved in year-round organizing around issues related to labour, immigrant rights, environmental justice, housing affordability, police accountability, fair taxation of business, community health, and environmental protection. The RPA is affiliated with Our Revolution.

Seattle People's Party

seattlepeoplesparty.com
Seattle, Washington State, US

The People's Party of Seattle is a community-centred, grass-roots political party led by and accountable to the people most requiring access and equity in the city of Seattle. The People's Party was formed by a coalition of grassroots organizers as a response to the election of Donald Trump and the corporatist Democratic politics which enabled him. At the request of the community, the People's Party put up Nikkita Oliver, an artist, lawyer, educator and grassroots organizer, in the 2017 mayoral election. She stood on a platform focused on affordable housing, mitigating gentrification and displacement, ending police brutality, and addressing homelessness, coming in a close third place. The People's Party prioritizes the needs of the people, especially those who are most marginalized, including women, people of colour, the LGBTQ community, immigrants, renters and the cash-poor.

While the People's Party acknowledges the often broken and corrupt nature of traditional politics, it understands that elections can be used by the people to transform institutions towards equity, justice and true democracy.

The People's Party was born from a profound and deep lack of trust in traditional politics, combined with the need and desire to be solution-builders. The People's Party strives to shorten the distance between politics and the people by building a political organization that is directly accountable to the people and communities. It recognizes that communities, especially those that are most marginalized, already have the answers to their own challenges and problems. For this reason it seeks to partner with the communities of Seattle to develop equitable political strategies and solutions which place people over profits and corporations.

The People's Party will continue to organize and develop and stand for future elections in Seattle, fighting for justice for all.

Take Back the City

London, United Kingdom

Take Back the City demands a fairer, better London for everybody. It aims to give political power to marginalized communities to create a democratic, diverse London. It does this by building power, using the resources already possessed – community, creativity and solidarity – and by taking power from big businesses and politicians who do not represent the people.

Established in 2015, Take Back the City is a growing group of disillusioned Londoners who got organized to tackle together the issues and injustices of life in the city. The platform undertook a big outreach process to understand more about what Londoners wanted to see change in their city. In April 2016, they turned these ideas and demands into a People's Manifesto, which group member Amina Gichinga used as a platform on which to run during the 2016 Greater London Authority elections. While she didn't win a seat, her campaign drew attention to the expensive housing, racist policing, the income crisis, and the despicable treatment of migrants and young people in London.

While Take Back the City is no longer a political party, it is still focusing its energies on building power in communities through listening to them and engaging with everyday issues in London. Take Back the City built local, living People's Manifestos in the run-up to local elections in May 2018, in order to hold politicians and local representatives to account for their promises. They are working to create a space for marginalized communities to give voice to their hopes, fears and ideas and to support them to fight against the systems that have marginalized them. Take Back the City is committed to equality for all and opposes all forms of oppression, whether on the grounds of race, sex, class, gender, sexuality, age or disability.

Terrassa En Comú
Terrassa In Common

terrassaencomu.cat
Terrassa, Spain

Terrassa En Comú is a municipalist platform which came into being, organized by activists from several social and citizen movements, in October 2014. The electoral programme of Terrassa En Comú was created through a participative process open to all citizens. The platform's political priorities include radical democracy and radical transparency, guaranteeing social rights, especially the right to housing, remunicipalizing the water supply and taking back control of public services while reducing the inequalities between districts. Terrassa En Comú took second place in the municipal elections of May 2015, receiving 16,000 votes, which translated into six councillors in the local government.

Terrassa En Comú is structured as a 'confluence' movement, bringing together individuals and members of local movements and political parties in a new project that gives priority to local issues. The activists of Terrassa En Comú participate in the movement in an individual capacity, rather than in the name of the group or organization to which they belong.

Terrassa En Comú was born from a desire to seize the moment, to read the signs and understand that the current time was exceptional, an emergency situation in which a serious response had to be formulated, and in which inertia would lead to paralysis. This context demanded a project focused on change, which would place political institutions at the service of the people.

València En Comú
Valencia In Common

valenciaencomu.org
Valencia, Spain

València En Comú is a municipalist platform based in the city of Valencia, which came into being at the end of 2014 with the support of various social collectives, and gained the support of Podemos for the May 2015 elections, in which it gained three key councillors and was a part of the movement that helped to end 24 years of Partido Popular government under Rita Barberá. For its candidacy at these elections, as well as for its daily activity, València En Comú works without any external financial support. Before the 2015 municipal elections it sold bonds to boost its collective financing; after the elections the value of these bonds was returned to those who had bought them. At the end of 2015, València En Comú established a study group, which aimed to draw up a programme of political action based on improving citizens' access to the city, as well as establishing a code of ethics that put into place, among many other elements, salary limits for elected officials in line with the average salary. The amounts saved on these salaries is used to finance social projects throughout the city.

Within the local government València En Comú co-ordinates the following areas: citizens' participation, rights and democratic innovation; education and youth issues; renewable energy and climate change; cultural activity; patrimony and housing. The three current councillors in the Municipal Group are María Oliver, Berto Jaramillo and Neus Fábregas.

The platform is structured as a meeting place for activists from a variety of social movements as well as members of Podem València. The various local groupings take place at neighbourhood or district level. Political activity is organized by a co-ordinating body made up of the three councillors, five people elected directly by the Plenario de València, and four elected by the Municipal Citizens' Council of Podemos València.

Vecinos por Torrelodones
Neighbours for Torrelodones

vecinosportorrelodones.org
Torrelodones, Spain

Vecinos por Torrelodones is a municipalist platform founded in April 2007 by a group of residents of Torredolones, a small town near Madrid with a population of 23,000. The group did not have any prior contact with politics, but were committed to their town, which had been governed by the same party (the conservative Partido Popular) for 25 years, and were concerned about the direction that municipal policy was taking. The group was particularly keen to stop a development plan for 3,500 homes and a golf course in an area of high environmental value, which had been protected by the 1993-97 city council in a unanimous decision.

In the first elections in which it stood, in 2007, Vecinos por Torrelodones won 23 per cent of the votes and four seats on the city council. In the 2011 elections it won 37 per cent of the vote and nine seats and formed a minority government. In 2015 the platform won 50.3 per cent of the vote, which equated to 12 seats, and was able to form a majority government.

The platform's key pillars are information, transparency, participation and 'transversality' (consensus-building) in local decision-making. It has moved council meetings from the mornings to the afternoons and started to broadcast them online in order to make them easier to attend or follow. It has established a department of resident services that responds to all the requests it receives from local residents (around 3,000 a year). The council's financial information is published online as open data so people can see how their taxes are being spent. It has promoted participation in policies relating to mobility, sport, the youth council, budgeting and urban planning.

Vila-seca en Comú
Vila-seca In Common

vilasecaencomu.org
Vilaseca, Spain

Vila-seca en Comú is a municipalist political platform made up of individual citizens with different origins, life-paths and affiliations, who decided to join together to create an autonomous political organization and run candidates at the municipal elections of May 2015. They wanted to move from mere indignation to the construction of a transformative alternative, so they built up a Group of Voters,[1] which came third in the elections.

They have shown since then that the creation of an open, participative, democratic, horizontal and transparent organization is possible. As is another way of doing politics – a way that is fairer and more socially committed.

They have established a political organization, built on citizens' assemblies, which is open to the population as a whole, made up of individual citizens and run by all those who participate in it.

In their work on the council, they have made human rights a priority, and they focus on a politics of social responsibility and sustainability. They promote activities aimed at guaranteeing social justice and financial redistribution within the sphere of the local government; they promote policies of efficient employment, for example by empowering social services, paying attention to dependent individuals, integration, healthcare, education and gender equality.

They try to make local government truly participative by decentralizing services, ensuring that decisions are taken by committee, supporting participatory budgeting and putting together a municipal action plan agreed on by the people as a whole and connected to social movements and the particular demands of people on the street.

---

1 Any group that collects a certain number of signatures of support (determined by the population of the municipality) can run for office as a 'group of voters' (agrupación de electores) for one term.

Fearless Cities

They have also worked to increase mobility within the city and remove architectonic barriers to improvement, thinking always of the needs of the population rather than private interests. They have actively collaborated to improve public transport and they carry on working to meet the needs of the population.

WeBrussels

webrussels.org
Brussels, Belgium

WeBrussels is a group of people fed up with the way mainstream political parties make decisions – with very little attention given to the wishes and inputs of citizens. This group wants to radically change this and bring about a system of deliberative democracy in Brussels.

Why WeBrussels? Because the current political system cannot deliver the society that citizens want to live in. Business as usual is simply not an option. They need to break with what they have, experiment and create something new.

WeBrussels is designing and experimenting with more flexible, responsive and transparent methods of democracy. Its processes intend to work with the communities it aims to support, and to capitalize on the incredible solutions and ideas produced and advanced by civil society and citizens alike. WeBrussels wants to be a participatory platform to empower citizen-led initiatives through the vote.

WeBrussels uses collective intelligence and a grassroots approach to empower anyone who joins the movement. It meets regularly to deliberate on individual initiatives and collective efforts, in order to work towards a common objective. Because of the idiosyncrasies of a city like Brussels (one of the most international in the world, and the 'capital' of the EU) they have also decided to focus significant efforts on attracting the 'expat vote', offering a new reason for voting to all the emigrants from around the EU and the world who converge here. WeBrussels want the expats thinking with us,

202

reimagining politics and taking municipalist ideas back home, so that they can spread and fuel the political revolution that Europe so desperately needs.

Working Families Party

workingfamilies.org
United States

Founded in New York in 1998 by a coalition of community organizations, union activists and progressive elected officials, the Working Families Party (WFP) today counts hundreds of thousands of individuals across the United States as part of its community. Since its support of the Bernie Sanders campaign, the WFP has continued to grow. It views electing the next generation of progressive leaders as a core area of its work.

The WFP is more than a pure municipalist platform, but since its founding many of its most high-profile victories have happened at the municipal level; from the rise of Bill de Blasio as the mayor of New York, to its campaign supporting the new progressive mayor of Albuquerque, New Mexico.

Some of its recent success stories have happened in cities around the American South, an area of the country with a long tradition of progressive and civil rights activism, but which often gets lumped together as 'Trump Country'. The WFP has been working with local activists in Southern cities, and recently played a part in progressive municipal election victories in Birmingham, Alabama; Jackson, Mississippi; Charlotte, North Carolina; and New Orleans. One Southern political observer even remarked: 'Probably the weirdest story of 2017: the Working Families Party is quietly becoming a major player in Southern municipal politics.'

Once the election is over what happens next? Progressive elected officials must be supported and provided with policy tools to enact progressive change. Therefore, the WFP encourages all of its elected officials to join Local Progress, the only network for progressive municipal elected officials in the country. Local Progress drives public policy on issues of economic justice, immigrant rights, racial justice and sustainability at the local level – an area of governance that is too often ignored by the progressive movement in the United States.

Zagreb je NAŠ!
Zagreb is OURS!

zagrebjenas.hr
Zagreb, Croatia

Zagreb je NAŠ! (ZJN) is a municipal political platform that emerged at the beginning of 2017. It is based on principles of social and political justice in a city aiming to bring together different left and green political parties and individuals in a joint attempt to enter the city assembly and consequently to build a leftwing political organization rooted in the city. It is built on the belief that the city should be governed by those who bear the consequences of political decisions and that city resources are to be used in order to better the life of its citizens, while producing the sense of self-governance.

In May 2017 ZJN formed a coalition with four other political parties: Nova ljevica (New Left), Radni ka fronta (Workers' Front), ORAH and Zagrad For The City. The coalition won four seats in the Zagreb City Assembly and 68 seats in neighbourhood and district councils all over the city. During the campaign the coalition also bore the name Zagreb je NAŠ!.

ZJN brings together individuals with backgrounds in the anti-privatization movement, labour activists, and public and cultural workers, as well as all those who wish to be active in their neighbourhood. It is structured through decision-making groups that are informed by working groups, with members overlapping. It has an executive group, plenum-like support groups and thematic working groups, as well as neighbourhood groups where platform members work directly with activists and engage in actions with people from the districts they are located in.

ZJN has been influenced and inspired by the emerging municipalist movement in Europe and the rest of the world. This also includes the aim of feminizing politics by including gender parity on its electoral lists and by promoting programmes that pay special attention to the rights of women, the LGBTIQ community and minorities.

Zaragoza en Común
Zaragoza in Common

zaragozaencomun.com
Zaragoza, Spain

Zaragoza en Común is a confluence movement of citizens, activists and political organizations, which came into being in 2014 as a part of the widespread movement to recover cities for their inhabitants.

Its structure includes a Citizens' Co-ordinating Group, Citizens' Plenary and Citizens' Assembly: Zaragoza En Común is divided into working groups, which are either local or thematic and which are always open and participative. These groups have formulated the group's electoral programme, along with the policies that since May 2015 have been put into practice by its Municipal Group in the Zaragoza city government. It works to harness the power of collective thinking, and aims to build the city of the future together.

Zaragoza En Común aims to create a new politics in the interests of the majority, free from the demands of the urban, financial and energy-providing oligarchs. The movement believes that it is in the city that change can start to appear and become effective, and that a democratic revolution can take place which will recover the city for its citizens, allowing them to live in it, design it, build it and govern it as citizens, generating a new way of living, a new way of using the city spaces, a new way of understanding the environment, a new culture. It is wellbeing and living well that should be the guiding principles of citizens' actions, which is why care and the sustainability of our life in the city are central to our political activities and the way in which we organize ourselves.

The model which Zaragoza En Común proposes to change the city is built around the struggle against inequality, support for public services, a local form of urbanism, the cleaning-up of public accounts, increased investment in non-central districts of the city, the struggle against climate change, increased participation and culture.

In a context of serious economic crisis, which has assaulted the city's economy since 2008, one of the main political goals of Zaragoza En Común is remunicipalization, allowing vital services to be controlled directly by municipal public administrations, which will lead to greater savings, higher quality of service and more jobs for the city. In Zaragoza, such an approach has met with great resistance from large companies, long-standing economic and media forces, and the political parties that serve their interests.

Acknowledgements

This publication is perhaps the most tangible manifestation to date of the global municipalist movement. Inspired by the Fearless Cities Summit held in Barcelona from 9 to 11 June 2017, it has been written collaboratively by 144 contributors from 54 towns and cities around the world, including mayors, councillors, grassroots activists and policy specialists. The International Committee of Barcelona En Comú, which co-ordinated this process, would like to thank the following people for their comments, constructive criticisms and contributions to the organizing and policy toolkits:

Adrià Alemany
Agnès Petit
Alberto de Nicola
Alberto Labarga
Alberto Recio
Alejandra Calvo
Alessandro
 Scarnatto
Álvaro Porro
Angelina Kussy
Angello Ponziano
Annie Morin
Antonio Calleja
Arturo Losada
Bea Martínez
Caio Tendolini
Carla Ruffini
Christopher Gepp
 Torres
Clare Walden
Cris Mañas
Daniel Cao
David Balbás
David Bravo
Elena Tarifa
Elisabet Sánchez

Eloi Badia
Emily Clancy
Enric Barcena
Enric Pons
Ercan Ayboga
Eric Recoura
Eunate Serrano
Federico Alagna
Federico Gatti
Francesc Magrinyà
Franco Ingrassia
Gabriela Alacid
Giulia Follo
Guilherme Serodio
Guy Oron
Iva Marcetic
Ivan Lam
Jaume Asens
Javier Miranda Baz
Juan Romero
 Raposo
Justina Koscinska
Kiki
Laia Bertran
Laia Rosich
Lara Salgados

Laura Calbet
Lucía Martín
Manuel Salinas
Mar Jiménez
Marcelo Expósito
Marie Depelteau-
 Paquette
Marina López
Marina Vicen
Mariona Pascual
Marta Cruells
Marta G. Franco
Marta Nalin
Marta Vallverdú
Mayo Fuster
Miguel Penas
Milica Lekovic
Monica Bertran
Nahum Mann
Nikita Bashmakov
Oriol Sorolla
Pedro Salinas
Peter MacFadyen
Rana Khoury
Raul Royo
Roberto Andres

Roberto Andrés
Sandra Salvador
Sarita Pillay
Sergi Caravaca
Sergi Cutillas
Sergio Espin
Silvia Giuntinelli
Sílvia Gla

Simon Thorpe
Simona Levi
Steve Early
Steve Hughes
Steven Forti
Susanna Segovia
Sylvia Fredriksson
Vanessa Maxé

Weronika
 Smigielska
Xabier Barandiaran
Ximo Balaguer
Xristina
 Moschovidou
Yagmur Sutcu
Ysabel Torralbo

Marta Junqué Surià deserves particular acknowledgement for her rigorous project management of the drafting and editorial process, and for her ability to convince us all that the book would see the light of day, even on the days when it seemed impossible. Thanks too, to the co-ordination team for its support in decisions relating to the editing of the guide, in particular Kate Shea Baird for her dedication to ensuring that the book met our expectations.

Special thanks go to First Deputy Mayor of Barcelona, Gerardo Pisarello, for his indefatigable commitment to the internationalization of the municipalist movement and his political support for the Fearless Cities Summit and for this book.

Last but not least, we would like to express our sincere gratitude to the following organizations for their support for the Fearless Cities Summit and guide, without which neither would have been possible:

- Charles Léopold Mayer Foundation
- Guerrilla Foundation
- European Culture Foundation
- Fundación Avina
- Karibu Foundation
- EDGE Funders Alliance

Index

Pagination in **bold** refers to a directory entry. *Italic* pagination refers to a key concept explanation.